Wage
and
Employment

Adjustment

---

in
Local
Labor Markets

Randall W. Eberts
Federal Reserve Bank of Cleveland

and

Joe A. Stone
University of Oregon

1992

W. E. UPJOHN INSTITUTE for Employment Research
Kalamazoo, Michigan

331.12 (handwritten)

Library of Congress Cataloging-in-Publication Data

Eberts, Randall W.
    Wage and employment adjustment in local labor markets / Randall W.
Eberts and Joe A. Stone.
        p.   cm.
    Includes bibliographical references (p.   ) and index.
    ISBN 0-88099-115-1. — ISBN 0-88099-116-X (pbk.)
        1. Labor market—United States.   2. Wages—United States.
3. Structural adjustment (Economic policy)—United States.
I. Stone, Joe Allan. 1948-   . II. Title.
    HD5724.E23   1992
    331.12'0973—dc20   91-41773
                                                                 CIP

Cover design by J.R. Underhill
Index prepared by Shirley Kessel
Printed in the United States of America on acid-free paper

Acknowledgments

In preparing this report, we benefited greatly from the comments, suggestions, and support of Patricia Beeson, David Blanchflower, Stephen Haynes, Louis Jacobson, Daniel McMillen, and Edward Montgomery.

The Authors

Randall W. Eberts is an assistant vice president and economist at the Federal Reserve Bank of Cleveland. He heads the research unit for applied microeconomics, regional economic analysis, and the computer systems support group. Prior to joining the Bank in 1986, he was an associate professor of economics at the University of Oregon. He has published numerous articles in academic journals on issues related to local public finance, public infrastructure, labor unions, and regional productivity and economic development. He is a frequent contributor to the Bank's publications, and has co-authored a book entitled *Unions and Public Schools* and co-edited two books entitled *Economic Restructuring of the American Midwest* and *Structural Changes in U.S. Labor Markets*. He earned his undergraduate degree from the University of California at San Diego and M.A. and Ph.D. degrees in economics from Northwestern University.

Joe A. Stone is W. E. Miner Professor of Economics at the University of Oregon. He received a Ph.D. in economics from Michigan State University in 1977, an M.A. in economics from Michigan State in 1974 (after service in the U.S. Army from 1970–1972), and a B.A. in economics from the University of Texas at El Paso in 1970. Professor Stone has previously served on the senior staff of the President's Council of Economic Advisers, as an Ameritech Fellow at the Center for Regional Economic Issues at Case Western Reserve University, as a senior research associate at the Federal Reserve Bank of Cleveland, and as a research economist at the U.S. Bureau of Labor Statistics. His research deals primarily with issues in labor and industrial relations and international economics and has appeared in a variety of academic journals, including the *Review of Economics and Statistics, American Economic Review, Journal of Political Economy, Economic Inquiry, Journal of Labor Economics,* and *Industrial and Labor Relations Review*.

CONTENTS

TABLES

FIGURES

1
Introduction

Metropolitan labor markets are in constant flux. At various times during the last two decades, different regions of the country have been bombarded by a variety of economic disturbances, or shocks. Oil price shocks, interest rate changes, technological advances, foreign competition, interregional migration, and foreign immigration have had significant and long-lasting effects on regional economies and their workers. These shocks have affected cities and their outlying regions in different ways and at different times. Some cities have experienced unprecedented growth from an increase in population or from an increase in the demand for workers. Other cities have undergone painful periods of employment loss and economic restructuring, cutting their economic base and displacing a large proportion of their workforce.

The severity of these disturbances on local economies depends on a host of factors: the linkage of the local economy with the rest of the country; the concentration of industries that are particularly vulnerable to national business cycles and longer-run structural changes; the ability of local industries to compete with other regions of the country and the rest of the world; and the ability of local workers to adjust to a changing labor market principally through retraining or migration.

Problems in Local Labor Markets

The contrast in performance of individual local economies resulting from these disturbances is striking, particularly within the last 10 years in which the East and West Coast economies have boomed while much of the middle section of the country has languished. The economic boom for cities on the West Coast, for example, was fueled to a large extent by the seemingly endless stream of migrants to California both from other

1

regions of the country and from other nations. Even the severe twin national recessions of the early 1980s, the worst since the Great Depression, were barely noticed by that region. East Coast cities boasted a similar growth spurt during the late 1970s and early 1980s, but for different reasons. The East Coast expansion was driven more by labor demand than by labor supply, as government demand for advanced military hardware escalated and the financial securities industry flourished.

Much of the rest of the country told an entirely different story. Texas and Louisiana cities, after riding high on the oil price increases during the mid-1970s, entered a severe recession in the early 1980s as oil prices plummeted. Cities in the farming states of the West North Central region experienced a similar fate entering the 1980s. Falling commodities prices, resulting from the national recession and from a weak export market, forced many farmers into receivership. In the Midwest, rapid technological changes and increased foreign competition had dire effects on the manufacturing sectors of various cities. Precipitated by the recessions of the early 1980s, Buffalo, Cleveland, and Pittsburgh, for example, lost as much as half of their manufacturing jobs as durable-goods firms in these areas found it difficult to compete with firms elsewhere in the country and in the world.

Significant adjustment in labor markets accompanied these episodes of economic disturbance. Workers moved from one region of the country to another in response to job opportunities, higher wages, and more favorable amenities. Displaced by economic restructuring, workers were forced to seek jobs in other sectors of their local economies, to move, or to face lengthy spells of unemployment.

Between 1979 and 1984, 5.1 million workers with at least three years of tenure lost their jobs.[1] The remaining 40 percent of these workers remained unemployed. Many, discouraged by poor job prospects, eventually dropped out of the labor force. Sixty percent were eventually reemployed, but upwards of 60 percent of these employed workers were forced to find jobs in industries other than the ones in which they were previously employed. Some sought jobs in other areas.

Economists and policymakers have taken a broad range of positions regarding the wide disparities in regional economic conditions. Some have credited the phenomenal increase in jobs over the last three decades to regional diversity, in which diversity offers ample opportunities for the kind of industrial restructuring necessary to promote future growth. According to this view, the reallocation of jobs across regions, in which regions gain and lose jobs depending upon their competitive advantage, is seen as a net gain to the U.S. economy. Others dismiss regional diversity as a temporary state of disequilibrium that will disappear as regional growth rates eventually converge through the migration of households and the location of businesses. If the disequilibrium effects of shocks on regions dissipate quickly through the adjustment of wages and employment, then there is little justification for public policy to promote firm location and household migration, except perhaps to enhance a region's physical and human capital. However, if the adjustment is protracted, then policies designed to ease the adjustment process are more justified.

Labor Market Adjustments
A Tale of Two Cities

The dimensions of these labor market adjustments can be illustrated more concretely by chronicling the experiences of two metropolitan areas that lie at opposite ends of the range of experiences. One city, Pittsburgh, experienced the pains associated with the downsizing of a key industry that for decades had been the foundation of its economy. The other city, San Jose, was faced with accommodating the explosive growth of an infant industry that eventually became for San Jose what steel had once been for Pittsburgh. While the transitions that these two cities underwent did not result from a sudden and unexpected shock, as was the case for some other cities, they do serve to underscore the salient features of the adjustments that occur within local economies.

For over a century, Pittsburgh was known as the nation's steel center. In 1950, for example, Pittsburgh produced 25 percent of the nation's steel output. This concentration came to an abrupt end in 1979, when U.S. Steel Corporation announced the permanent closing of 12 plants. Within three years, employment in these plants fell from 22,554 to 8,000 and the area's total employment in primary metals was cut 36 percent. Today, Pittsburgh produces only 10 percent of the nation's steel and employs only 7 percent of the nation's steelworkers.[2]

The tremendous downsizing of the industry quickly spilled over into much of the rest of Pittsburgh's economy, which was so closely linked to steel. Between 1980 and 1983, during the depths of the recession, 57,000 manufacturing jobs were eliminated, half of which were in primary metals. As the recovery generated steam to become the longest peacetime expansion since World War II, it became evident that the loss of steel production and of manufacturing jobs in general was not merely a cyclical event. By the end of the decade, Pittsburgh proceeded to lose another 15,000 steel jobs and another 36,000 manufacturing jobs, bringing the total number of lost manufacturing jobs to 93,000.

The transition was painful for many labor groups in the Pittsburgh community. The unemployment rate soared to over 14 percent during the first two years of 1980. This level exceeded the national unemployment rate by 40 percent. Many workers, particularly the younger and more highly skilled, left the region. During the 1980s, Pittsburgh experienced the greatest population loss among the 23 largest metropolitan areas in the United States. Those manufacturing workers who remained behind were not readily absorbed into other sectors. For those who could find jobs, overall job quality deteriorated, and half of the reemployed displaced workers earned less than they had in their previous jobs.

During the decade, other sectors within Pittsburgh's economy stepped in to replace the 93,000 jobs lost in manufacturing. The metropolitan area gained 74,000 jobs in services, 26,000 in wholesale and retail trade, and 9,000 in finance, insurance, and real estate. By the end of the decade, Pittsburgh had managed to replace the 93,000 lost manufacturing jobs with private sector jobs from these various other sectors. While in many respects this was a remarkable feat, Pittsburgh's overall employment growth during the heart of the national expansion (1983 to 1987) was still the lowest among the nation's 23 largest metropolitan areas. Only Houston, which was particularly hard hit by low oil prices, had lower employment growth during this period. As a result of this restructuring, Pittsburgh's economy shifted from 30 percent of employment in manufacturing in 1980 to only 14 percent in 1989.

The story of San Jose is the tale of the birth and development of a new industry, the computer and semiconductor industry.[3] In some respects, the growth of San Jose and the semiconductor industry in the years after World War II is reminiscent of the growth of Pittsburgh and the steel industry at the turn of the century. Prior to World War II, the San Jose area was a sparsely populated agricultural valley, which for the most part was detached from the large urban areas of San Francisco and Oakland lying to the north. The seed for the growth of the area and current dominance of the electronics industry was planted during and immediately after the war when a few electronics companies established operations in the area in order to gain access to war-related markets and to be close to the research taking place in and around Stanford University. Since then the area's population has increased by almost a million people, and 350,000 new jobs have been created, of which over 33 percent are in electronics-related companies. Most of the country's semiconductor companies can trace their roots to this area.

Because of the rural origins of the region, workers for the electronics industry, many of whom were engineers and technicians, came from outside the area. Much of the adjustment San Jose has faced has been in accommodating the streams of newcomers and the congestion and social problems that followed them. The area constantly confronted shortages—in workers, in housing, and in adequate infrastructure.

Total employment in the San Jose metropolitan area increased 53 percent between 1975 and 1986. Interestingly, population increased by only 17 percent. The difference was made up almost entirely by an increase in the percentage of the working-age population actually employed, swelling from 46 percent in 1975 to 57 percent by 1986. The increase in labor force participation alone could have accounted for half the increase in employment, without one additional worker moving into the area or any change in the unemployment rate. In comparison, assuming the same population size and labor force participation in 1986 that existed in 1975, the reduction in the unemployment rate, resulting from tight labor market conditions, added only 4 percent more workers. Even though more individuals joined the labor force, pressure on the local labor market pushed wages from 10 percent above the national average in 1975 to 20 percent above the national average by 1986.

Institutional factors and local development initiatives played significant roles in the labor market adjustments of both cities. For Pittsburgh, several factors have been cited as affecting the transition. The high degree of unionization was said to be a barrier to labor adjustment. Unions were blamed for impeding the substitution of various types of workers and the substitution of capital for labor. Unions also exacted a wage premium, which can raise the cost of production if not accompanied by higher productivity. Opponents of unions argued that the relatively higher production costs discouraged firms from locating or expanding in the area and prompted some firms to leave.

Many have argued that Pittsburgh's transition was aided by several local development efforts. The Allegheny Conference, under an initiative known as *Strategy 21,* set out to promote economic development by improving labor force skills and training, converting underutilized resources to new uses, enhancing the region's quality of life, and expanding opportunities for women, minorities, and the structurally unemployed. Pennsylvania's Ben Franklin Partnership for Advanced Technologies, initiated in 1982, was an active partner in promoting high-tech development in the area by supporting entrepreneurial development and by allotting funds to train displaced workers for high-tech jobs.

The initial stimulus for the development of the electronics industry in the San Jose area had its origins in government initiatives. These activities included opening a military technical training facility at a nearby naval air station and infusing large amounts of federal funds for basic electronics research and development at Stanford University. In addition, several local communities in the area established industrial parks that provided land, financial assistance, and infrastructure benefits to attract electronics industries. More recent local government programs have been directed toward problems resulting from too much growth, such as housing shortages, congestion, and poor air quality. For instance, in the 1970s Santa Clara County legislated public controls over industrial growth—one of the first such measures in the country.

While more dramatic than the experience of many cities that faced economic restructuring, the adjustment process in Pittsburgh and San Jose may be typical in many respects. Unfortunately, little is known about the dynamics of wage and employment determination in local labor markets. What are the relative roles of migration, changes in unemployment, and changes in labor force participation in the adjustment of a region's labor supply following economic shocks? Conversely, what are the relative contributions of business births and deaths, expansions and contractions to changes in labor demand? How elastic are demand and supply curves for labor in major metropolitan labor markets? How long does it take for wages and employment to respond to supply and demand shocks? Do public policies (for instance, local public expenditures, including public sector infrastructure investments) make a difference to local wage and employment determination? These questions are important for understanding the workings of local labor markets and assisting policymakers in constructing and implementing programs that may address the labor adjustment issues that continue to face so many metropolitan areas.

The importance of understanding the adjustment process in order to implement effective state and local economic development policy cannot be understated. Many such policies have been implemented with a quick fix in mind. Constrained by the short political horizons facing elected officials, many states and localities have sought to address long-term adjustment problems with short-term remedies. One of the most prevalent, and possibly least effective, is the strategy popularly known as ''smokestack chasing.'' In recent years the strategy has taken on an international dimension with Japanese or other foreign transplant facilities having become the coveted prize. However, communities that pursue such strategies and offer substantial subsidies to entice companies to locate within their jurisdictions may find that in the long run the costs outweigh the benefits. Furthermore, these communities may be ignoring the very reasons for lackluster growth in their areas, such as poor infrastructure and an inferior educational system, which eventually may cause the businesses that they have convinced to move in to leave.

Outline and Major Conclusions

The objective of this study is to provide a deeper understanding of the processes by which local labor markets adjust to economic disturbances and the potential role for public policy in improving local labor markets. We begin chapter 2 by specifying a general framework for analyzing supply and demand behavior in local labor markets. Changes in the supply of labor are divided into three major components: changes in the unemployment rate, changes in labor force participation, and migration flows. An increase in labor demand presumably will offer more job opportunities to the unemployed, increase the incentive for individuals to enter the workforce and search for jobs, and entice workers from outside the region to seek employment within the local economy.

The process and speed of adjustment to an external shock depends on the relative contribution of each of these components to the change in the labor supply. The composition of change in the labor supply also influences the extent to which the indigenous population is affected by an economic shock, and, consequently, the efficacy of public policy. For instance, suppose a local government offered generous public subsidies in an attempt to combat chronic high unemployment by attracting new businesses. The success of the program would depend not simply on the number of new jobs generated but also on who filled them. If most of the jobs are snatched up by workers from outside the area, then the subsidy program has largely missed its mark, except for the secondary effects induced by the injection of new jobs.

Labor market adjustments also take place on the demand side. Regions with a large influx of households, such as the Southeast and the West Coast, attract new businesses. While service-related businesses are the most obvious ones to be sensitive to population increases, manufacturing firms are increasingly locating near market areas, as production becomes more customized and just-in-time inventory control requires closer proximity to suppliers. Therefore, we would expect openings of new firms to be an important component of the labor market adjustment process.

In addition, labor demand is also a source of shocks to the local market. Identifying the relative contribution of the components to a net change in labor demand helps to isolate the source of these disturbances. Four components are identified: openings, closings, expansions, and contractions. By comparing the rate of job creation (openings and expansions) to the rate of job destruction (closings and contractions), one can get a sense of the reallocation of jobs within an area and, consequently, the change in employment opportunities.

In chapter 3 we extend our analysis first by describing specific types of economic disturbances, which include technological changes, sharp changes in oil prices, monetary policy, and government spending and taxation. We next bring to focus existing evidence on how wages, employment, and unemployment in local labor markets adjust to those disturbances.

In chapter 4 we establish an empirical framework for estimating the relationships between wages and employment and present estimates of dynamic supply and demand relationships based upon data from 21 metropolitan areas during the period 1973 to 1987. We also present estimates for the separate goods and service sectors that include interactions between the two groups of industries. We use these estimates to simulate the wage and employment responses to demand and supply shocks to understand the properties of the dynamic adjustment.

In chapter 5 we test for the influence of specific local factors on metropolitan labor markets, including rates of unionization, government taxation, and investments in public infrastructure (e.g., roads, bridges, street lights, schools, hospitals, sewers, and airports). With regard to unionization, we are interested in the possible effects of unionization on both the levels of labor supply and demand in local labor markets and the responsiveness of labor supply and demand. For example, are higher rates of unionization associated with lower elasticities of labor supply?

With regard to government policies, we are interested in the familiar issues related to the effects of taxation on local labor supply and demand, and also in the importance of investments in local public infrastructure. Recent work suggests that public infrastructure investments play a key role in urban economic development, but fiscal pressures on a wide array of other budget priorities have led many cities to neglect investments in infrastructure. How serious are the consequences of this neglect?

A final chapter summarizes and evaluates our major conclusions. To briefly preview those conclusions, we find evidence in support of the following:

1. In the course of a year, the largest component of change in local labor supply in recent years has been change in labor force participation, rather than in unemployment rates or migration.

2. In the course of a year, the largest component of change in local labor demand in recent years has been change in the openings of new firms, rather than closings, expansion, or contractions.

3. Wage differentials among cities are much more persistent over time than unemployment rate differentials, which tend to erode over periods as short as a decade.

4. Labor supply and demand tend to exhibit a recursive structure, with firms initially adjusting employment rather than wages in response to economic disturbances.

5. Labor supply and demand responses are elastic, but protracted, so that full adjustment to a major economic disturbance takes more than a decade.

6. In the course of adjustment, both wages and employment tend to "overshoot" the new equilibrium. For example, in response to a negative shock, local economic conditions get much worse before they get better.

7. In the separate goods and service sectors of local economies:
   (a) Labor demand is more elastic in the goods sector than in the service sector.
   (b) Labor supply is nearly perfectly elastic in the separate sectors.
   (c) Job reallocation between the two sectors accounts for much of the protracted response of the local labor market to a disturbance.
   (d) Expansions in the goods sector induce a modest increase in the service sector, but expansions in the service sector tend to "crowd out" employment in the goods sector.

8. Unionization is associated with a decline in overall labor demand and a decline in the speed of the response of overall labor supply.

9 . High local taxes, holding investments in public infrastructure constant, tend to *decrease* both labor supply and labor demand.

10. Increased investments in local public infrastructure, holding local taxes constant, tend to *increase* both labor supply and labor demand.

NOTES

1. See Flaim and Sehgal (1985).
2. Employment data are from Bureau of Labor Statistics, *Employment and Earnings.*
3. See Saxenian (1984) for a description of the emergence of the Silicon Valley.

2

A Framework for Understanding Local Labor Market Adjustment

Local labor markets are bombarded by a continuous stream of anticipated and unanticipated changes in the supply of and the demand for labor. Sources of these changes can come from within or from outside the regional economy. Some events are more easily identified than others. For example, abrupt oil price increases, such as that following the Iraqi invasion of Kuwait in August 1990, command immediate attention, and their starting points are easily recorded. Less observable, but no less important, are the slower and more subtle effects that come from the adoption of a new technology or from a shift in a region's international comparative advantage resulting from exchange rate movements. Regardless of the source, a shock to a local labor market prompts an adjustment that may be quick or protracted depending on the fundamental characteristics of workers and firms in a local economy and its linkages with other regional markets.

The starting point for understanding the local labor market adjustment process is the basic supply and demand model of a labor market. In this neoclassical view, wage and employment outcomes are viewed as the result of an auction between buyers and sellers of labor. Typically, buyers are business establishments, and sellers are households. This invisible auction is characterized by flexible wages that are driven toward an equilibrium level that equates the quantity of labor demanded with the quantity supplied. Therefore, absent any external shocks to a local labor market or to changes in worker preferences or workplace conditions, wages and employment settle down to specific levels.

The purpose of this chapter is to examine what happens when this equilibrium state is disturbed. After describing the rudimentary workings of local labor markets according to the neoclassical view, we will explore various ways in which local labor markets respond to market

13

disturbances. The responses are divided into those originating from households and those originating from businesses. Household responses are further separated into three basic components; changes in employment resulting from shifts in unemployment, changes in labor force participation, and changes in population from migration. Business responses include employment changes resulting from openings, expansions, closings, and contractions of firms. This chapter provides estimates of the relative magnitudes of these responses in order to gain a perspective on how metropolitan labor markets adjust to shocks.

General Characteristics of Labor Supply and Demand

Individual labor supply is determined by decisions of individuals to allocate their fixed amount of time between leisure and work. Many factors enter into this decision: the wage offered, workplace conditions, fringe benefits, worker preferences, and nonlabor income. An aggregate local labor market is comprised of individuals with different characteristics and preferences and, thus, changes in the labor market elicit different behavior. As the factors listed above vary, individuals may decide to enter the labor force, unemployed workers may choose to intensify their search effort, employed workers may work additional hours, and workers may seek employment opportunities in other regions. In the aggregate, these individual responses are manifested in changes in labor force participation, unemployment rates, hours worked, and migration.

Labor demand for individual firms results from a business's input decisions. Since labor is essential to producing any good or service, the demand for labor is closely tied to the demand for a firm's products. In addition, the demand for labor is influenced by the state of technology, the quality of the worker, costs of other inputs, and the way management combines these inputs with labor. In response to an increase in output demand, a firm employs additional workers until the cost of hiring the last worker (or of expanding the hours worked) equals the value of the worker's contribution to the production of output. Furthermore, an increase in market wages causes a firm to cut back on employees to the extent that it can hire other relatively cheaper inputs that can substitute for labor's contribution to output. Over time, businesses locate in an area that enables them to maximize long-run, after-tax profits.

The purpose of this simple model is to aid in understanding how local markets respond to changes in the factors that affect labor supply and demand. We begin the description by focusing on a single labor market in an aggregate economy. We assume that a given region trades with other regions and that workers can freely migrate in and out of a region. Referring to figure 2.1, this labor market is initially in equilibrium at point A, where the wage level is w_0 and the employment level is E_0.

Suppose that the demand for a region's product declines as a result of changes in factors exogenous to that region. As a result, the demand curve shifts inward and to the left. It may be possible that firms could accurately predict the length and depth of the decline in product demand and cheaply store the goods (or services) for future sale. If this were the case, then a temporary reduction in product demand would not necessarily lead to a decline in labor demand. However, it has been the experience of modern developed economies during business cycles that labor demand is closely tied to product demand, and we still adopt this stylized fact.

The leftward shift of the labor demand curve indicates that firms would like to either reduce wages at the initial level of employment (E_0) or reduce employment at the initial wage level (w_0). If wages adjust slowly, or are rigid downward for institutional reasons, such as union contracts or minimum wage laws, the initial effect is excess labor (E_0–E_2) at w_0. Unemployment increases, and employers fill vacancies on the basis of factors other than wages, such as seniority or worker quality.

If wages adjust, then the excess labor supply pushes wages down through the auction process of a spot market until the quantity of labor demanded and supplied is equated once again. With reference to figure 2.1, the new equilibrium occurs at E_1, which represents a reduction in the level of employment from the initial equilibrium state.

How does this reduction take place? First, firms and workers may cut back on the hours worked each week, by reducing overtime or resorting to shortened shifts. Second, firms may actually lay off workers, either

Figure 2.1
The Effect of a Reduction in Labor Demand
on the Labor Market

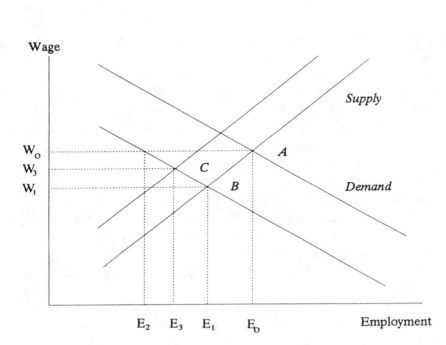

permanently or temporarily, until product demand recovers. Third, to the extent that real wages fall, some workers may no longer find it desirable to work and, thus, voluntarily leave the labor force. Fourth, individuals may actually move to another area in search of better job opportunities.

In the neoclassical view, labor flows are highly responsive to spatial wage differentials. Regions with excess labor supply, evidenced by high unemployment, are characterized by low wages, and regions with excess demand, measured by low unemployment, are characterized by high wages. Migration presumably flows from low- to high-wage regions, reducing but not necessarily eliminating regional differences in unemployment and wage rates.

As we explore in the next chapter, the speed and efficiency of adjustment is a topic of recent inquiry and debate. Furthermore, some researchers have questioned whether wages are sufficiently flexible downward in order to bring about equilibrium. Instead of responding to wage differentials alone, it has been postulated that workers respond to job opportunities, as reflected in a region's unemployment rate. Both cases move a region's labor market toward equilibrium.

Composition of Labor Supply Responses

Adjustments in local labor supply can come about in four ways: (1) a change in the number of hours worked, (2) a change in unemployment, (3) a change in labor force participation, and (4) a change in population resulting from migration. The relative magnitude of these reactions to employment shocks has important implications both for the nature and speed of the adjustment process and for identifying the individuals most affected by the shocks. Therefore, we examine the motivating factors behind these separate responses, categorize the population groups that are most affected by each respective response, and document evidence on the relative efficiency and speed of adjustment for each component. Last, we provide empirical evidence that suggests that of the components considered, changes in labor force participation dominate the labor supply response in local labor markets. In the discussion to follow, we exclude the number of hours worked because available data pertain only to manufacturing workers, and because evidence suggests that little of the change in aggregate labor input comes from a change in the length of the workweek.[1]

Migration Decisions

The U.S. population is relatively mobile, certainly more so than in most other developed countries. Household migration decisions are based on a host of factors: demographics, wages, job opportunities, local amenities, government services and taxes, climate, culture, and proximity to family. Of these factors, age has consistently been shown to be the single most important factor in determining who migrates. Studies show that the peak mobility years are ages 22 to 24, when nearly 20 percent of this age group migrates across county or state lines. By age 30, only 10 percent of this population segment migrates. Education is the single best predictor of who will move within an age group. However, it is not simply more education that increases the likelihood of a move; rather, it is a college education, *per se,* that makes migration more likely.

Migration is responsive to local economic conditions as well as to personal characteristics of the labor force "at risk" to migration.[2] Individuals are more likely to leave an area with high unemployment than an area with low unemployment. Furthermore, a higher percentage of migrants are unemployed than are nonmigrants, suggesting that being without a job motivates workers to look elsewhere for work. Yet, the relative success rate of those looking for employment was smaller for migrants than for nonmigrants. This also suggests a speculative behavior on the part of migrants in moving to a region without first securing a job. Ideally, households weigh the relative merits of relevant regional attributes and decide accordingly. Unfortunately, some information is not easy to obtain, and households face decisions with only partial knowledge.

In addition to imperfect information about the current state of a region, labor market conditions constantly change. Households have no guarantees that seemingly desirable conditions will last long enough for a move to be worthwhile. Consequently, expectations of future labor conditions among regions are an important element in the labor market adjustment process.

Topel (1986) incorporates expectations of future conditions into his model of household migration. However, instead of treating future events with uncertainty, he assumes that workers fully anticipate future demand shocks. Under this assumption, he estimates that a positive transitory labor demand shock reduces, not increases, current local wages. He explains this departure from previous research by postulating that expectations of future demand, based on current conditions, induce workers to move to an area ahead of realized demand. The resultant influx of workers in excess of what current demand can absorb, lowers wages. This overshooting persists until expectations fall back in line with actual conditions.

Another characteristic of migration patterns is that not all households are equally likely, and capable, to migrate. Most migration studies find that older and less-skilled workers—the ones most likely to be displaced by structural change—are the least mobile. Flaim and Sehgal's (1985) finding that less than 2 percent of displaced workers leave the area in which they have lost their jobs is consistent with this picture. Consequently, workers who are left behind bear the largest cost of negative employment shocks in local labor markets. Topel finds that wages vary most among groups of workers with the least mobility. In times of economic prosperity for a region, these same immobile workers may not reap the full benefit of the upturn because workers from other areas, who are presumably more qualified, quickly move into the region and claim the newly created jobs.

However, the less-skilled and thus less-mobile labor groups may not be totally disenfranchised. Bartik (1990) suggests that a one-time positive demand shock may have more permanent effects on unemployment rates than one might expect. Bartik adopts the notion of "hysteresis," in which a positive shock to a local labor market could cause a sufficient enough shortage of skilled workers within a region that firms are forced to hire workers with fewer skills than they otherwise would under normal conditions. The short-run employment experiences change these individuals' values, skills, self-confidence, and reputation. As a result, these workers are better able to compete with inmigrants and, consequently, are more likely to find employment in the long run and more likely to be employed in a higher-paying job.

Job Search

Describing the movement in and out of unemployment entails both an explanation of job-search behavior and of the reasons for voluntary and involuntary unemployment. The literature on these topics is voluminous, and for our purposes it is sufficient to say that these decisions are also based on relative costs and benefits. Employee-initiated decisions to search or to quit voluntarily are based on factors similar to the ones weighed in describing migration. Relative wages, opportunity cost of working, and job opportunities are the most important factors. The latter behavior is evident from findings that quit rates are high when labor markets are tight and when jobs are plentiful relative to job-seekers. The issue of involuntary unemployment will be taken up later.

Labor Force Participation

Recent research reveals three core factors that explain much of the interregional variation in labor force participation. Gallaway, Vedder, and Lawson (1991) use data from 50 states for the years 1982 and 1985 to explain regional variation in the change in labor force participation. They find that participation is higher in states with higher wages, lower transfer payments, and lower unemployment rates. In addition, labor force participation is slightly higher in states with right-to-work laws and a greater proportion of the labor force unionized. Therefore, to a large extent, labor force participation works in the same direction as migration: regions with higher wages will attract more workers from other regions and draw individuals into the labor force.

Speed of Adjustment

The speed of adjustment of local labor markets depends in part on the relative contribution of each of these sources of labor supply response to shocks. Presumably, the search cost in time and money is lowest when one searches locally. Therefore, one would expect that local markets that depend the most on changes in unemployment rates would have the quickest response. Changes in both labor force participation and migration, however, involve more complex decisions, which take longer to complete than is typically the case with changes in unemployment.

Despite the relatively large cost of collecting information about job prospects in other regions and the costly process of actually changing locations, interregional labor migration has received considerable attention as an equilibrating mechanism.[3] However, the efficiency of interregional migration as a mechanism to reallocate labor geographically has recently been called into question.

A recent volume of studies by Van Dijk et al. (1989b) on migration and labor market adjustment generally points to a slower-than-expected local adjustment process. If migration does not respond quickly to changes in labor market conditions, then the adjustment process may depend more heavily on adjustments of the unemployment rate and labor force participation. Moreover, wages are more sensitive to employment shocks. Consequently, workers who are idled by the misfortunes of a negative employment shock in one region could be employed in another region, if it were not for the physical and psychological costs of relocating.

The consensus view among these studies is that local labor markets are generally in equilibrium, or can quickly return to equilibrium when shocked out of it. This view is brought into question by recent research by Greenwood et al. (1990). Using the general equilibrium framework described at the beginning of the chapter, they postulate that equilibrium exists when net migration between regions is zero. To test this hypothesis, they first estimate a net migration model in which the wage level is one of the explanatory variables. Next, for each region, they solve for the wage level that would force net migration to zero. Comparing this calculated wage with the actual wage for each region, they conclude that a majority of states are in disequilibrium. This finding suggests that migration is either too slow an adjustment mechanism or that not enough migration occurs, as a result of high mobility costs or institutional factors that impede local labor markets from quickly returning to equilibrium.

Pissarides and McMaster (1990), examining regional labor markets in Great Britain, also find slow adjustment in response to regional unemployment rate differentials, although there is adjustment to the compensating equilibrium. The authors estimate this dynamic relationship by regressing the adjustment of relative wages on unemployment differentials for the nine regional groupings in Great Britain during the period 1961–1982. Their long-run estimates imply that relative wages compensate for unemployment differences at the rate of three to one. For example, if a region's unemployment rate is 1 percentage point above the national average, its wage rate would be 3.2 percent above the average wage rate for the country as a whole. This result is consistent with the positive correlation between wages and long-run unemployment found by Adams (1985) and Marston (1985) for U.S. labor markets.

However, Pissarides and McMaster extended the analysis to examine the effects of shocks on wages and employment and found the adjustment to be slow and not monotonic. For example, if a shock disturbs the equilibrium in relative wages at given employment ratios, the estimated process closes only half of the initial disequilibrium after 12 years. Compensating equilibrium is not achieved until 20 years after the initial shock. Vanderkamp (1989), estimating the regional labor market adjustment process for Canadian provinces, also finds a fairly slow and complex adjustment path of employment, although he does not offer an estimate of the actual length of time.

Estimating the Composition
of Labor Supply Responses

To understand the method by which local labor markets reestablish equilibrium, who is affected by the adjustment process, and the speed of adjustment, it is necessary to estimate the relative contribution of the three components to short-run changes in the labor supply.[4] Their relative roles in the adjustment process of local labor markets can be estimated by following the methodology used by Houseman and Abraham (1990). They separate employment changes into the three labor supply components by first defining employment in a local labor market as:

$$E = P * LF * (1-U), \qquad (2.1)$$

where E is employment, P is population, LF is labor force, and U is unemployment. The percentage change in employment can then be written:

$$e = p + lf - u. \qquad (2.2)$$

where the lower case letters refer to percentage changes of the variables listed above. Metropolitan area unemployment rates are measured as annual averages; labor force participation rates are defined as the percentage of the population in the labor force; and population is based on annual estimates from 1975 to 1986, except for 1980 when actual census figures are used.[5]

Several different samples and specifications are estimated in order to gauge the robustness of the results. The first sample includes annual data between 1975 and 1986 for all 305 Standard Metropolitan Statistical Areas (SMSAs), as defined in 1981. Estimates of the response of the three supply components to employment change are derived by regressing changes in the rates of these components, as described in equation (2.2), on the rate of total employment change and year and regional dummy (0–1) variables. The change in total employment is presumed to reflect changes in labor demand, which induces these labor supply responses.[6]

Results, shown in table 2.1, suggest that the change in labor force participation accounts for the largest proportion of the change in the labor supply. Three-quarters of the percentage change in employment is attributed to individuals entering and leaving the labor force. The percentage change in unemployment and the percentage change in population equally share the remaining 25 percent of the percentage change in total employment.

The large role of labor force participation in the short-run local labor supply response is somewhat surprising. One would anticipate that the primary response for local labor markets would be migration. Indeed, Houseman and Abraham (1990), using annual state-level employment data for the years 1978 to 1985 and following the identical methodology, found migration to play a large role, particularly for males. Unfortunately, their study and ours are not completely comparable, since they estimated separate response equations for males and females. Houseman and Abraham found that, for males, population change accounted for

Table 2.1
Labor Supply Response to Changes in Total Employment

Model	Unemployment	Labor supply components	
		Labor force participation	Population
(1) All SMSAs, 1975-1986, labor force with total population	.134 (24.41)	.756 (104.07)	.110 (20.15)
(2) All SMSAs, 1980-1984, labor force with ages 15-64 population	.218 (18.38)	.592 (44.41)	.191 (19.82)
(3) All SMSAs, 1980-1984, labor force with total population	.218 (18.38)	.614 (47.17)	.168 (17.19)

SOURCES: U.S. Department of Labor, Bureau of Labor Statistics, and U.S. Department of Commerce, Bureau of Economic Analysis.
NOTE: Year and regional dummy variables are included in the regression equations.

half the labor supply response to employment change. Labor force participation accounted for only 30 percent and unemployment accounted for 18 percent. They found that labor force participation was appreciably more important for women, accounting for 57 percent of the change in employment, while the population response accounted for only 33 percent. Obviously, even Houseman and Abraham's estimate for the female participation rate response does not equal the magnitude we found for the entire sample.

Several differences between our sample of metropolitan areas and their sample of states, and between our measurement of these supply components and theirs, may shed some light on the differences in the two sets of results. Before trying several refinements, it should be noted that labor force participation rates vary considerably across Standard Metropolitan Statistical Areas (SMSAs), ranging from 28 percent in Jacksonville, North Carolina, to 66 percent in Iowa City, Iowa, in 1986. Furthermore, while the average participation rate has risen over the 12-year period, increasing from 42.7 percent in 1975 to 48.8 percent in 1986, the standard deviation has remained relatively constant, around 5.02. Unfortunately for purposes of comparison, similar statistics were not presented in the Houseman and Abraham paper.

The first difference between our estimates and theirs is the measurement of regional unemployment rates. We used unemployment rates estimated jointly by the Bureau of Labor Statistics and state employment agencies. Houseman and Abraham derived unemployment estimates directly from the *Current Population Survey* (CPS) tapes. Estimates directly from the surveys are typically much more volatile than those derived jointly, which could account for the larger role of unemployment found by Houseman and Abraham.

The second difference is the measurement of labor force participation. Data limitations forced us to use the entire population to compute labor force participation, while they used the typical working-age population. However, working-age population estimates were available in our dataset between 1980 and 1984, and labor force participation rates were reestimated using population between the ages of 15 and 64. Under this definition, the participation rate averaged 71.3 percent compared to an average of 47.4 percent for the same period when the entire population was used to compute the rate. Estimates based on this refined defini-tion and using the shorter time period still show labor force participa-tion to be the largest of the three labor supply components, accounting for 60 percent of the percentage change in total employment. Unemploy-ment accounted for 22 percent, and population change accounted for 17 percent.

The reduction in the estimated role of labor force participation under the revised definition resulted almost entirely from using the time period between 1980 and 1984. Using the original definition of labor force participation, which contained the entire population in the denominator, yielded almost identical results when estimated for the years 1980 to 1984. Consequently, the choice of the population measure to define labor force participation made no significant difference to the regression results.

Another explanation of the differences in results is that our sample is possibly biased because we included a large number of relatively small metropolitan areas. To see how sensitive our results are to the size of the SMSA, we estimated the labor supply response equations using a sample of the 40 largest SMSAs for the period 1975 to 1986. Our estimates reveal that the labor force participation rate response was smaller for the sample consisting of larger SMSAs than for the sample of all SMSAs (58.8 percent versus 75 percent). Nonetheless, participation rate response still dominated the other two labor supply responses, although the population and the unemployment response increased, amounting to 21.4 percent and 19.8 percent of total employment change. The greater importance of population change in larger cities is under-standable and consistent with findings in the labor migration literature that households are attracted to larger cities because of their greater employment opportunities and enhanced amenities.

Finally, we explored the use of population change as a proxy for migra-tion. Both our study and the one by Houseman and Abraham used the same measure of population change. Yet, it may be the case that popula-tion change is not as accurate a proxy for net migration flows at the metropolitan level as it is at the state level. Using data on migration flows and on birth and death rates, we found that virtually all of the variation in population change across SMSAs resulted from variation in net migration flows. The standard deviation of the percentage change in population from migration was 3.5 times greater than the standard deviation of the percentage change in population from births and deaths. Although the migration series is not long enough to provide good estimates of the supply response equation, the fact that migration explained a large share of the population change placed more confidence on population as a good proxy for this component of labor supply.

Variation in the Composition of Labor Supply Across Regions

Local labor market characteristics differ considerably across regions. For example, the southern and western portions of the country have the allure of a mild climate and presumably would be marked more by inmigration than cities with less attractive climates. To identify regional differences in metropolitan labor markets, we estimated the supply component equations for metropolitan areas within each of the nine census regions. As shown in table 2.2, while there is variation across regions in the relative magnitude of the three components, labor force participation still dominates in all regions. Yet, the relative magnitudes across regions of the individual components offer interesting insight into the workings of these regional labor markets. For example, unemployment rates carry the most weight in the East North Central states, a region that has undergone significant restructuring, particularly within manufacturing. Therefore, one would expect the many displaced workers to be reflected in unemployment rates, as the estimates suggest.

With respect to population change, two of the regions experiencing the most migration and the greatest population growth, the South Atlantic and the Mountain states, yield the largest estimated weights for population change. At the same time, the contribution of labor force participation to labor supply responses is the lowest among the regions.

Labor force participation is the most important source of labor supply change in the West North Central region. This area is characterized by a stable population base, which traditionally has depended upon agriculture. Since farm employment is not included in total employ-

Table 2.2

Variation in the Composition of Labor Supply Changes Across Census Regions

Census region	Unemployment	Labor supply components	
		Labor force participation	Population
New England	.109	.838	.053
Middle Atlantic	.162	.758	.080
East North Central	.271	.656	.073
West North Central	.023	.956	.021
South Atlantic	.125	.652	.223
East South Central	.219	.710	.071
West South Central	.168	.708	.124
Mountain	.161	.612	.228
Pacific	.100	.742	.158

SOURCES: U.S. Department of Labor, Bureau of Labor Statistics, and U.S. Department of Commerce, Bureau of Economic Analysis.

NOTES: Year and regional dummy variables are included in the regression equations. All coefficients are statistically significant at the 1 percent level.

ment, workers leaving the farm to seek work in other sectors would increase the labor force participation rate. Furthermore, it appears from the low weight on the unemployment rate that most workers leave the farm only when they have secured a job elsewhere.

Summary

Contrary to other studies, our estimates suggest that adjustments in labor force participation are the primary means by which regional labor supply responds in the short run to shocks. The relative weights of the three labor supply components vary across census regions, and in ways that are consistent with the dynamics of each region. The estimates highlight the asymmetry in response across regions to labor demand shocks. For example, the neoclassical model would predict that the large number of displaced workers resulting from the shakeout of manufacturing would migrate to regions with greater job prospects. However, we find that the contribution of population change to the labor supply response in the East North Central region (a region with net outmigration) is half the magnitude of its contribution in the Pacific region and one-third that of its contribution in the South Atlantic region (both regions experience net inmigration). Instead, these displaced workers remain in the region and swell the unemployment roles. Therefore, our estimates suggest that the large role given to migration to equilibrate regional markets may be overstated. However, our results do point to the possibility that the indigenous population may benefit from an increase in demand more so than if most new jobs were filled by migrants.

Composition of Labor Demand Shifts

Jobs are continually being created and destroyed within local labor markets as a result of cyclical and structural changes brought about by one or more of the various types of shocks. Most studies consider only the net effect of this dynamic process, but the real drama lies in the gross flows of jobs created through firm openings and expansions and jobs lost through firm closings and contractions. These gross flows are quite substantial. Estimates from various sources indicate that it is not uncommon for as many as one-third of the jobs in a local labor market to change hands during any two-year period.

Our purpose for looking at the components of the change in labor demand is to understand more fully the factors that drive the realloca-tion of employment positions in the local labor market and thus the area's employment dynamics. To the extent that shocks to local economies originate primarily on the demand side, these components also reveal the channel through which these disruptions are transmitted through the labor market. For instance, does a negative labor demand shock come primarily from a sharp increase in closings or contractions of existing firms or from an abrupt decline in openings or expansions? Converse-ly, does a positive demand shock come more from the opening of new firms or from the expansion of existing firms?

Firm and Establishment Level Databases

Only recently have these questions been explored empirically by look-ing at job turnover within and between industries. In order to address these issues, employment information for individual firms is required. Currently, three sources of such information are available. The first is the Small Business Administration's (SBA) extract of *Dun and Bradstreet* data. *Dun and Bradstreet* collects information periodically for roughly 5 million establishments across the United States in order to assess a business's credit quality. The Small Business Administra-tion uses the *Dun and Bradstreet* data to construct a longitudinal dataset of establishments from all industrial sectors starting from the mid-1970s.

A second source of establishment-level data is the *Longitudinal Research Dataset* (LRD), which is a matched file of manufacturing establishments derived from the Census and Survey of Manufacturers. Although this database is limited to only manufacturing, its advantage is that the information is probably more reliable since it is more fre-quently updated and accurately checked than the SBA data. Moreover, this database has more information about establishments than simply employment.

The third source is a series of monthly establishment surveys (referred to as ES202 files) conducted by state employment security bureaus to provide estimates of employment changes. These files are considered relatively accurate because states use this information to track unemployment insurance taxes paid by firms. Therefore, states have an incentive to be certain that the information is current. The major drawback of this dataset is that it contains only employment figures, and that only a handful of states have allowed researchers to access the otherwise confidential establishment-level records.

The Job Reallocation Process

The question we want to explore related to labor demand response is analogous to the question on the labor supply side: what is the relative importance of the four components of labor demand in responding to shifts in demand? Stated slightly differently, what are the primary factors that explain intermetropolitan differences in net employment change?

In many respects, answers to these questions go to the heart of the economic development process. Is it the case that one regional economy grows faster than another because it creates more jobs or because it destroys fewer jobs than another region? If a region is growing faster because it is creating new jobs faster than another region, then it is more than likely that these new firms are introducing new products and new technologies to a region's industrial base. However, if a region excels in employment growth because fewer jobs are being destroyed, then even though the region is growing it is not adding to its stock of technology and products at a greater rate, which may have implications for the region's future growth.

A growing number of studies have estimated the creation and destruction of jobs with the development of various datasets mentioned above (Baldwin and Gorecki 1990, chapter 9). These studies have examined this reallocation process from many different dimensions: over time, across industries with different overall growth rates, and across regions with different growth rates. The traditional view of the job reallocation process is that sunk costs would induce job destruction through the exit of firms insensitive to business cycle downturns. When deciding to enter a market, a business must anticipate covering average cost while existing businesses, which already have their capital in place, only have to cover marginal cost. Thus, cyclical changes in market demand would affect the decision to start a business more than the decision to close a business. Consequently, job creation would be expected to vary more than job destruction.

However, recent research, using both the LRD and ES202 data, contradicts this standard view of entry and exit. For instance, Davis and Haltiwanger (1990) find that for manufacturing firms recessions are associated with large increases in job destruction and only small decreases in job creation. Leonard (1987) finds similar results using *ES202* for establishments in Wisconsin. Jacobson (1986), on the other hand, finds exit rates to be more stable than entry rates between 1976 and 1985 for western Pennsylvania, using state unemployment insurance files.

The issue we want to explore is a longer-run relationship across regions. A scenario similar to the temporal one could apply to regional economies. A region grows because its resources and other attributes are attractive to businesses. Because of the region's comparative advantage, firms remain competitive and eventually expand. In this case, the creation of jobs, both from openings and expansions, would be positively related to the net employment growth of a region. The destruction of jobs is related to structural effects that are relatively constant across regions.

The alternative hypothesis is that the creation of jobs remains constant across regions, and the destruction of jobs varies. Regions with the highest growth rates lose the fewest jobs through closings or contractions, and vice versa. Consequently, the percentage of jobs lost from closings and contractions is negatively related to the net employment change across regions.

The evidence is much more supportive of the "creation" view of economic development across regions than for job reallocation over time. Most studies that address this dimension find the variation in regional net employment change to be principally the result of differences in rates of births and expansions. Rates of employment loss, from both deaths and contractions, are quite constant across regions.[7] These results are consistent with other studies based on different datasets.[8]

Metropolitan-Level Estimates

Previous studies consider rather broadly defined regions, however. Since the focus in our analysis is on local labor markets, we examine the job reallocation process at the metropolitan level. Our findings, based on SBA data, are consistent with these studies in that the gross labor flows within local labor markets are substantial, and are much greater than the net flows. As shown for a representative sample of metropolitan areas in table 2.3, the gross flows are as much as 10 times the magnitude of net flows.

Furthermore, these flows are large for even the slowest growing metropolitan areas. For example, table 2.3 shows that within the two-year period between 1984 and 1986, an estimated 22.6 percent of total nonagricultural jobs changed hands in Akron, even though net employment grew only 0.46 percent. Moreover, the sum of the percentage of jobs created and destroyed within the same two-year period equaled 44.8—a substantial amount of job reallocation.

A large proportion of this job reallocation came from openings and closings. Akron's employment increased by 16.20 percent due to openings, but at the same time Akron lost 13.99 percent of its employment base due to closings. Columbus, on the other hand, experienced a 15.90 percent net increase in employment over the same time period, with the percentage of jobs gained from openings twice the percentage of jobs lost from closings.

The relative contributions of the four components averaged for all metropolitan areas are displayed in table 2.4. Jobs gained from openings exhibited the largest variation among the four components, measured by the coefficient of variation, which is the standard deviation divided by the mean. Jobs lost from closings had the least variation. These results strongly suggest that net employment change is largely attributable to job creation.

To estimate the correlation between each of the four components and net employment change, we followed the same procedure used for labor supply. Each of the four components were regressed on net employment change and regional and time dummy variables. Three time periods are considered: the expansion period of 1976 to 1978, the recession

Table 2.3
Composition of Changes in Labor Demand for Selected Metropolitan Areas, 1984–1986

Metropolitan area	Net employment change	Percentage employment change originating from			
		Openings	Expansions	Closings	Contractions
1. Akron	0.46	16.20	6.43	-13.99	-8.18
2. Anaheim	6.88	19.44	11.42	-18.26	-5.72
3. Atlanta	15.58	22.18	12.61	-14.65	-4.55
4. Baltimore	8.93	19.00	10.82	-15.62	-5.27
5. Birmingham	8.73	21.12	10.25	-15.51	-7.13
6. Buffalo	2.57	15.36	7.26	-14.63	-5.42
7. Chicago	5.54	16.31	8.83	-13.67	-5.92
8. Cincinnati	3.16	13.27	8.25	-13.54	-4.82
9. Cleveland	0.64	13.31	8.48	-15.17	-5.98
10. Columbus	15.90	20.47	9.74	-9.56	-4.75
11. Dallas	5.68	20.03	10.44	-16.68	-8.10
12. Denver	6.16	20.18	8.87	-15.16	-7.72
13. Detroit	0.97	13.20	8.96	-15.40	-5.80
14. Greensboro	13.24	17.21	9.34	-8.73	-4.57
15. Houston	-5.41	16.75	7.54	-20.91	-8.80
16. Indianapolis	8.70	17.64	10.09	-11.05	-7.98
17. Kansas City	4.28	16.26	8.24	-14.76	-5.46
18. Los Angeles	3.95	16.78	9.78	-17.10	-5.52
19. Miami	2.18	15.48	8.72	-16.39	-5.63
20. Milwaukee	4.36	13.57	7.96	-11.71	-5.45
21. Minneapolis	15.29	19.42	11.22	-9.82	-5.53

22. New Orleans	0.86	15.41	6.03	-13.94	-6.65
23. New York	0.61	12.64	8.33	-15.38	-4.98
24. Newark	7.18	16.36	8.88	-12.61	-5.45
25. Philadelphia	-6.16	15.54	10.01	-13.87	-5.52
26. Pittsburgh	-8.19	11.46	5.82	-13.76	-11.71
27. Portland	5.43	20.12	8.14	-13.15	-9.68
28. Rochester	19.33	29.66	7.13	-12.12	-5.35
29. St. Louis	8.19	16.48	8.62	-11.72	-5.20
30. San Diego	19.36	27.32	12.93	-15.63	-5.26
31. San Francisco	2.26	13.48	8.81	-14.27	-5.76
32. San Jose	7.50	19.19	10.74	-16.21	-6.21
33. Seattle	11.08	21.58	10.02	-13.87	-6.65
34. Tampa	8.68	20.73	9.89	-17.25	-4.70

SOURCE: U.S. Small Business Administration, U.S. Establishment Longitudinal Microdata (USELM).

Table 2.4
Labor Demand Response to Net Changes in Total Employment

Variable	Labor demand components			
	Openings	Expansions	Closings	Contractions
Coefficient on net employment change	.43	.34	.09	.14
(*t*-statistic)	(24.8)	(24.2)	(6.1)	(11.6)
Sample mean	13.30%	11.42%	-11.14%	-7.58%
Sample standard deviation	7.01	5.71	4.21	3.32
Coefficient of variation	.53	.50	.38	.44

SOURCE: U.S. Small Business Administration, U.S. Establishment Longitudinal Microdata (USELM).

period of 1980 to 1982, and the expansion period of 1982 to 1984. The size of the estimated coefficient indicates how much each component is correlated with net employment change. For example, a large positive coefficient associated with firm openings compared to a coefficient of zero for firm closings would suggest that employment growth is attributable to firm openings, while firm closings are invariant to the rate of employment growth within a metropolitan area.

The results, shown in table 2.4, provide additional support for firm entries being the primary force behind regional employment growth. The coefficient on openings is five times the coefficient on firm closings. Furthermore, although the coefficient on firm closings is statistically significantly different from zero, its magnitude is very close to zero, which means that jobs lost due to closings is invariant to regional growth conditions. The same holds true for jobs gained from expansions relative to jobs lost from contractions, although the difference in the size of the coefficient between the two components is not as dramatic.

These results preserve to some extent the Schumpeterian notion that growth is associated with a bunching of new product introductions. However, the relative constancy of the percentage of jobs lost due to destruction appears to suggest that adverse regional shocks slow business formation more than increase business destruction. Labor demand shocks appear to affect firm openings, possibly through technological, exchange-rate, and monetary shocks. Therefore, the pivotal point in distinguishing between growing and declining metropolitan regions is firm openings and expansions. Growing metropolitan areas, relative to declining areas, tend to have a large proportion of jobs created from firm openings. This view is consistent with the firm-level results that the entry (and exit) of establishments is highly correlated with the variability of sales around a trend growth rate (Baldwin and Gorecki 1990, chapter 9).

Relative Importance of Shifts in Demand and Supply

The dynamic behavior of local labor markets is revealed in the interrelationship between wage changes and employment changes. Before estimating these relationships in chapter 4, it is instructive to examine these shifts over time and across metropolitan areas. Wage rates of individual employees are aggregated for each of a sample of large metropolitan areas.[9] Through regression techniques and information on individual worker's education and experience, we are able to construct a wage rate that reflects the wage paid to a typical worker. More specifically, by controlling for differences across metropolitan areas in a worker's characteristics, we essentially place the same worker in each labor market and observe the wages received by this typical employee.

Aggregate Employment and Wage Changes

A sample of 21 SMSAs is used in this analysis for reasons related to data limitations, described in the data appendix. Percentage changes in wages and employment for the 21 SMSAs relative to percentage changes in national wages and employment are displayed in figure 2.2. Total employment in the 21 areas has lagged behind the national rate throughout most of the time period. However, employment trends appear to be counter to the national business cycles. During national economic expansions, the SMSAs' growth rate fell below the nation's, while during the recession years (1980–1982), the employment growth rate exceeded the national rate. Much of this countercyclical behavior can be attributed to the goods-producing sector, which exhibits wide deviations from the national growth rates (figure 2.3). For instance, between 1983 and 1987, goods-producing employment grew at most at a rate 5 percent slower than the nation, while service employment grew at most at a rate 2 percent below the national rate (figure 2.4).

Employment changes in the service-producing sectors of these 21 SMSAs do not deviate as sharply from the national employment changes as do the goods-producing sectors. However, these sectors also lag behind the national growth rates for most of the period, even during the last expansion period.

After some brief gyrations between 1974 and 1976, wage growth within the 21 SMSAs has gradually approached the national pace, and has consistently exceeded the national rate throughout the current expansion. This higher-than-average wage growth results primarily from

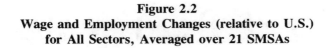

Figure 2.2
Wage and Employment Changes (relative to U.S.)
for All Sectors, Averaged over 21 SMSAs

Percentage Change

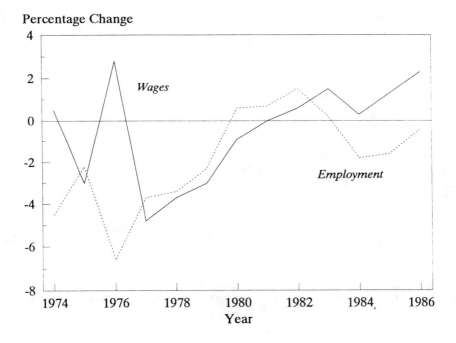

SOURCE: BLS Household and Establishment Surveys.

Figure 2.3
Wage and Employment Changes (relative to U.S.)
for Goods Sector, Averaged over 21 SMSAs

Percentage Change

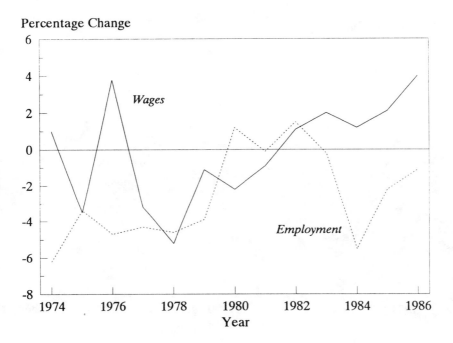

SOURCE: BLS Household and Establishment Surveys.

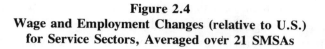

Figure 2.4
Wage and Employment Changes (relative to U.S.)
for Service Sectors, Averaged over 21 SMSAs

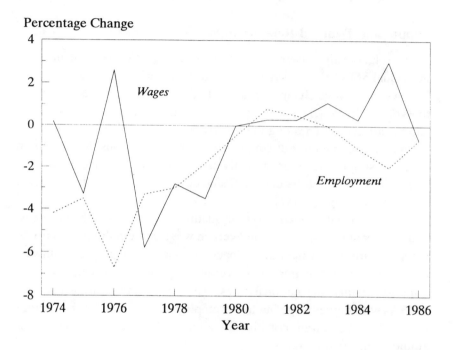

SOURCE: BLS Household and Establishment Surveys.

a rapid rise in manufacturing wages, relative to the nation. Although service-sector wages have exceeded the national rates in recent years, the differential averages less than 1 percent. Service wages have also lagged behind national wage increases, except in the most recent years.

Supply and Demand Relationships

The relationship between wage changes and employment changes for individual SMSAs averaged over various time periods is shown in figure 2.5. Average wage changes (relative to the nation) are measured along the vertical axis, while average employment changes (relative to the nation) are measured along the horizontal axis. One can interpret this scatter plot as tracing out supply and demand relationships. Shifts in the labor supply curve, presumably caused by shocks, trace out the demand curve, while shifts in the demand curve, also the result of shocks, identify the supply curve.

The plot can be divided into four quadrants, as shown. The northeast quadrant contains SMSAs with average wage and employment growth rates that are higher than the respective national rates. The southwest quadrant contains the areas with average wage and employment growth rates lower than the national rates. The southeast quadrant contains SMSAs with higher wage but lower employment growth rates, whereas the northwest quadrant contains the areas with lower wage but higher employment growth rates.

Combining these quadrants in various ways reveals several characteristics of the 21 SMSAs. Employment growth for nine SMSAs exceeded on average the national rate throughout the 15-year period. These SMSAs are all located in the West and South except for Columbus and Nassau-Suffolk. Ten SMSAs experienced positive wage changes (relative to the nation), on average, between 1973 and 1987. All but two of these, Akron and Cincinnati, are located in the West.

The relative positions of the SMSAs within these four quadrants reveal a strong positive correlation between changes in wages and employment. For example, two-thirds of the SMSAs lie in the northeast or southwest quadrants, which indicates that a positive wage change is associated with a positive employment change (or a negative wage change

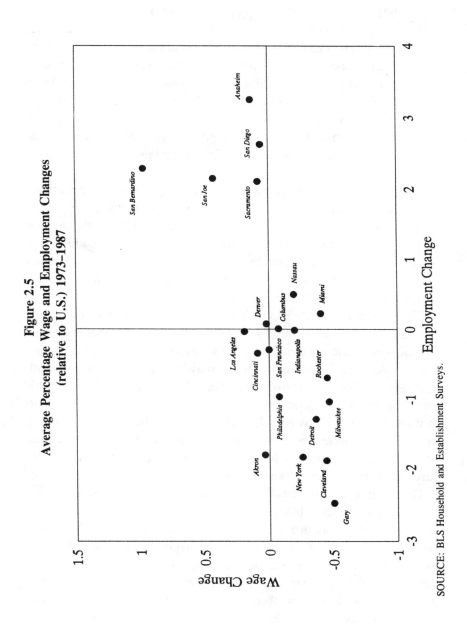

Figure 2.5
Average Percentage Wage and Employment Changes
(relative to U.S.) 1973–1987

SOURCE: BLS Household and Establishment Surveys.

with a negative employment change). However, there are some notable exceptions, such as Los Angeles, Miami, and Cincinnati, which exhibit negative correlations between changes in wages and employment.

The significance of the negative correlations can be understood by thinking of the plots as describing the intersections of individual supply and demand curves—an intersection for each SMSA. The identification of supply and demand curves is discussed in chapter 4. For now, the general pattern of equilibrium points is suggestive of the relative importance of demand and supply shifts in explaining local labor market dynamics.

For example, the preponderance of observations within the northeast and southwest quadrants can be viewed as being situated along a common supply curve, which has been traced out by shifts in the demand curve. The shifts can come about from shocks to the demand for labor. As mentioned earlier, examples of demand shocks include the entry or exit of businesses into an area, public infrastructure projects, and productivity changes.

The fact that not all SMSAs lie in the northeast and southwest quadrants suggests that shifts in the supply curves may also be important in describing local labor market dynamics. For areas such as Miami, Cincinnati, and Los Angeles, labor supply shocks may be the primary determinants of changes in local labor markets. These shocks may result from rapid inmigration (or outmigration) of workers, which is particularly important for Miami and Los Angeles. They may also be caused by various government policies, such as differences in unemployment insurance or welfare qualifications, which may influence participation in the labor force by various segments of the population.

The relative importance of demand and supply shocks in describing the dynamics of local labor markets may also be seen in the relative dispersion of points around the origin. Points in the northeast and southwest quadrants are farther from the origin than points in the other two quadrants. If we were to superimpose a supply and demand curve that splits the points into four equal groups, the supply curve would lie primarily within the northeast and southwest quadrants. More than likely the supply curve would lie near San Jose on the one end and Gary-Hammond on the other end. The demand would probably be situated near Nassau-Suffolk and Cincinnati. In this case, we would notice that the points lie closer on average to the supply curve than to the demand curve. Consequently, the relatively greater dispersion around the demand curve than the supply curve suggests a more prominent role for demand shocks in local labor markets than supply shocks, although both are important. Work by Beeson and Eberts (1989) supports this finding that both demand and supply factors are important, but the demand side seems to be more prevalent.

The service-producing and goods-producing sectors yield similar patterns of points within the four quadrants (not shown). However, for the service-producing sector the clustering of points around a hypothetical supply curve is not as tight as was observed for either both sectors together or the goods-producing sectors alone. This suggests that the dynamics of the service sectors may be balanced more evenly between demand and supply factors.

To summarize, examination of wage and employment changes for a sample of metropolitan areas reveals that the dynamics of these labor markets approximate, to some extent, the predictions of a simple neoclassical model. The plot of employment and wage changes resembles the supply and demand curves typically drawn for markets. Moreover, the plots are consistent with exogenous factors shifting the supply and demand curves, with shifts in demand dominating.

Conclusion

We began the discussion of the mechanics of local labor market adjustments with a simple neoclassical model in which markets clear through wage and employment changes. However, even though employment is the appropriate "quantity" variable to use in estimating the dynamics of local labor markets, it veils the workings and relative contributions of various components of labor supply and demand in the market adjustment process. Estimates revealed that short-run adjustments in labor supply, in response to demand shocks, result primarily from changes in labor force participation.

Migration is also an important adjustment factor, but its contribution is dwarfed by labor force participation, even within regions that had experienced tremendous growth during the sample period. This is not to say that regions with high growth have not benefited from migration. Rather, the results suggest that there is a more pronounced difference in the change in labor force participation among regions with different rates of employment change. Changes in labor demand across regions are attributable mainly to regional differences in the percentage of jobs gained from business openings. Putting supply and demand together, we found that shifts in demand appear, on average, to dominate changes in wages and employment for most cities.

NOTES

1. As reported in Kniesner and Goldsmith (1987), evidence from the aggregate U.S. economy during recessions suggests that the dominant portion of typical demand-induced reduction in the aggregate labor input is a decline in the number of employed workers in the form of layoffs, rather than a significant shortening of the average workweek.

2. Van Dijk et al. (1989b) provide compelling evidence for these relationships.

3. For an early survey of this literature, see Greenwood (1975).

4. Hours worked is the fourth component, but it will not be considered in the analysis, since these data are availble only for manufacturing workers, while unemployment rates and population change are not available for manufacturing workers but only for total local labor market.

5. The typical definition of the labor force participation rate restricts population to the ages between 16 and 65. This information was not available for all years, but was available for a shorter time period. Estimates using this population age group were qualitatively the same as estimates using the entire population, presumably reflecting the little relative change in the age distribution across metropolitan areas.

6. Houseman and Abraham also employ an instrumental variables approach in an attempt to separate demand effects from supply effects. We did not attempt this approach for two reasons. First, they found that the estimates derived from the two methods were not qualitatively different. Second, we intended our inquiry to be merely suggestive of the relative contributions of these three components to the labor supply response.

7. A recent paper by Dunne, Roberts, and Samuelson (1989) compares the gross flows of manufacturing employment from each of the four components between contracting and expanding regions. They find very little difference in the percentage of jobs lost from both closings and contractions between these two types of regions, although job destruction was slightly higher in contracting regions.

8. See Baldwin and Gorecki (1990) for a review of these studies.

9. The data appendix describes the data sources and methodology in greater detail.

3

Shocks to Local Labor Markets

Chapter 3 lays the groundwork for interpreting estimates of the dynamic adjustment patterns of labor markets to be presented in chapter 4. To do this, we delineate the types of shocks that may affect regional labor markets, highlighting what we know about the market adjustment process gleaned from previous studies. We also consider characteristics of local labor markets that may affect the speed of adjustment in responding to a shock and emphasize the evidence of the gradual adjustment, or persistence, of, first, wages and then unemployment rates. We also look at the relationship between wages and unemployment and the way in which each contributes to the adjustment process.

Shocks

A shock is an event that alters the current equilibrium position of a market. In our specific case, it alters the steady-state growth path of each regional labor market. What are these events that shift demand and supply sufficiently to push regional and national economies away from their steady-state growth paths? Shocks may originate either inside or outside a region. Examples of exogenous shocks include sudden swings in oil prices, increases in foreign competition, alterations in state and federal governments' taxing and spending policies, shifts in the age and other characteristics of the regional labor force, innovations in industrywide technology, and fluctuations in the aggregate demand for a region's products. Internal shocks may come from new technology development and implementation specifically within a region, increased worker quality gained through worker training initiatives, change in union representation, improvement in labor-management relations, or enhancement of a region's amenities such as public infrastructure investment. These internal events can be specific to a particular region or sector. External events, such as oil price shocks, monetary policy changes, or state and federal tax and expenditure changes, can affect more than one region or sector simultaneously, although the net result might differ by region and sector.

Technological Change

Technological change is generally considered a slow and gradual process that affects regional growth by altering the comparative advantage of sectors within a region. By making one sector more competitive than another, technological change shifts demand among sectors and regions, increasing demand in one sector sometimes at the expense of another. New techniques and products are continually being introduced. Some are more successful than others, and thus vary in their economic impact. Historically, the development of mass-produced automobiles, various farm implements, chemical products and processes, and polymers have launched several industries, along with the regions housing them, into prominence. In recent years, the microprocessing-chip revolution has transformed many industries and sectors. The phenomenal growth of the Silicon Valley and Boston's Route 128 areas has directly resulted from this new technology.

Many state and local economic development strategies have tried to capitalize on potential innovations for their own areas. A recent report released by the Ohio Edison Program—a state-funded agency that promotes, among other things, technology transfer—lists several new technologies that may have potential for transforming Ohio's industrial base. Many of these future technologies are largely extensions of those already in practice. However, the report foresees several that are presently not essential to Ohio industry, but will become critical in the 1990s. These include areas of biotechnology and bioengineering, particularly related to Ohio agribusiness. The use of lasers in industry, with applications in cutting, measuring, and surface treatment promises to transform Ohio's machine tool industry. Also, plastics may replace steel in automobile bodies, and miniature computers may replace manual controls, according to the report.[1]

Some innovations listed in this report have already affected industries within the Midwest, which in turn can impact the geographic distribution of manufacturing in the United States. For example, innovations in polymers and plastics have increased their use in products that once were made primarily of steel, such as large applicances and automobiles. As a result, the steel industry has experienced a significant reduction in demand for sheet metal products. Regions that have been heavily dependent upon steel, such as Pittsburgh and Gary, have suffered large employment losses in steel and related industries because of these structural changes in demand.

A convenient and commonly used measure of process-oriented technological change is the change in output minus the change in share-weighted private inputs, referred to as Solow residuals or multifactor productivity (MFP). This measure counts everything not included in changes in labor and private capital inputs as contributing to changes in productivity. In addition to changes in inputs other than labor and private capital, this measure could include, among other attributes, research and development expenditures, quality of workers, managerial skills, and public infrastructure investment. National level estimates of the annual change in MFP show a marked variation in multifactor productivity over time.

Obviously, events that happen at the national level will happen in at least one region and industry. Conversely, if enough regions share in episodes of economic upturns and downturns, then these may generate national business cycles. Hulten and Schwab (1991) constructed manufacturing MFP measures for the nine census regions for the period 1965 to 1986.[2] They found substantial variation in the annual growth rate of MFP among the various census regions. However, this variation is modest compared with that in the growth of labor and private capital. Therefore, Hulten and Schwab concluded that MFP is not the primary cause of regional differences in manufacturing output growth.

Similar measures, shown in table 3.1, constructed for a sample of 40 metropolitan areas for the period 1965 to 1977, exhibit variations in growth rates for MFP and labor and private capital for those metropolitan areas that are similar to Hulten and Schwab's. The same conclusion is drawn: regional differences in input growth, not in MFP growth, explain most of the regional variations in manufacturing output.[3]

Table 3.1
Regional Differences in Productivity (and Components)
1965-1977

		Average annual growth	
Variables	**All**	**Snowbelt**	**Sunbelt**
Output	2.82	2.36	3.54
MFP	1.41	1.57	1.18
	(50.0)	(66.5)	(33.3)
Private capital	1.24	.80	1.93
	(44.0)	(33.9)	(54.5)
Labor (hours)	.17	−.005	.44
	(6.0)	(.4)	(12.4)
Labor productivity	2.42	2.35	2.54

NOTES: Growth rates are computed by averaging the annual growth rates within each time period. Labor is computed as the number of hours worked during the year, as described in the text. Labor and private capital are weighted by their share of total output, assuming constant returns to scale for the private inputs. Numbers in parentheses are the share of the growth rate of output for each component: MFP, private capital, and labor.

Oil Prices

Regional economic fluctuations could also be caused by broader but more temporary factors. A sudden change in oil prices is one example of broader factors that hit regions simultaneously. With well-integrated oil markets and the relative ease of transporting the commodity, one would expect that oil price shocks are likely to occur simultaneously and be of roughly equal magnitude across regions. Since oil is so widely and intensively used, a steep price rise would increase the cost of production, which would induce businesses to cut back on production. Hamilton (1983) demonstrates the pervasiveness of oil price shocks and contends that most of the recessions since World War II were immediately preceded by such an event.

As a result of differences in industrial composition and relative industrial productivity, regions may be affected differently by sudden oil price changes, and recent research, by Bauer and Byrne (1991) for example, supports this view. As expected, higher-priced oil boosts gross state product (GSP) for the largest oil-producing states. Alaska's and Wyoming's economies appear to benefit the most (table 3.2). Texas and California are also large oil suppliers, but the beneficial effects of higher prices to these regions were dampened because their economies are more developed and less dependent on the oil-producing sector. States with large manufacturing bases and heavy reliance on agriculture and forestry appear to be most adversely affected by oil price shocks. Manufacturing is hit by higher oil prices because of its heavy petroleum use as an input in manufacturing. Both agriculture and forestry are adversely affected because of their intense demand for oil in transportation.

Table 3.2
Ranking of States by Net Effect of High Oil Prices
on Growth Rate of GSP

Top ten		Bottom ten	
State	Net effect	State	Net effect
Alaska	0.79	Oregon	−0.21
Wyoming	0.43	Georgia	−0.21
Louisiana	0.32	Florida	−0.21
Oklahoma	0.24	Massashusetts	−0.22
New Mexico	0.17	Hawaii	−0.22
Texas	0.16	South Dakota	−0.22
West Virginia	0.01	Maryland	−0.22
North Dakota	−0.02	Rhode Island	−0.23
Montana	−0.02	Michigan	−0.28
Utah	−0.02	Arizona	−0.30

SOURCE: Bauer and Byrne (1991), used with permission.
NOTE: Numbers reflect the impact of a 1 percent increase in oil prices on real GSP growth.

Monetary Policy Shocks

Monetary policy surprises are another example of shocks that hit regions simultaneously and have widespread but possibly regionally different effects. The twin recessions of the early 1980s were for the most part caused by the monetary policy mistakes of excessive money growth during the previous decade. The shock produced by a disinflationary policy that policymakers believed was necessary to get the economy on an acceptable real growth path left 46 of the 48 contiguous states with year-over-year employment losses at some point between 1980 and 1982. It is interesting to note that even though monetary policy is ubiquitous across regions, its effect differed regionally, as evidenced by the different times at which states entered and left the recession, and the relative severity of regional downturns.[4]

Government Finance and Expenditures

With government purchases of goods and services accounting for over 20 percent of gross national product (GNP), government spending can have a significant effect on economic activity. This effect can vary across states for two reasons. First, federal dollars are not evenly distributed geographically. Recent procurement figures illustrate the high regional concentration of government military spending, for example. Northeastern and West Coast states were the primary recipients of defense dollars during the 1980s, generating, in part, the economic boom experienced by both economies during this period.[5] Conversely, defense cutbacks have been one of the reasons cited for the prolonged recession in the Northeast since 1989.

Second, state and local government spending also varies by state. Measured relative to GSP, table 3.3 shows how the size of the public sector ranges from 10 percent of GSP for Texas to 22.4 percent for Alaska. The average for all states is 15.8 percent. States with the largest public sector tend to be concentrated in the Northeast and to some extent in the Pacific region. States with the smallest public sector are found in the East South Central portion of the country and up through the Midwest.

States also vary in the composition of their public sector. The largest portion of state and local government expenditures goes toward education, with an average of 6.2 percent of GSP. Spending on education ranges from a high of 9.9 percent of GSP in North Dakota to a low of 3.6 percent in Louisiana. Capital outlays, the next largest component of state and local government, average 3.4 percent of GSP. They also vary substantially across states with the maximum share at least twice as large as the minimum share.

The variation in state and local government spending, particularly with respect to capital outlays and education, has significant implications for regional economic growth. Recent research on the effect of public infrastructure on economic development suggests that local public infrastructure is a positive and significant input in a region's production process, and attracts firms and households to an area.[6] The issue of the effect of public infrastructure on local labor market dynamics is explored in chapter 5.

State and local tax structures also affect regional economic performance, primarily through their effect on the location of firms. Empirical evidence of this relationship is limited, since the ability to track firm mobility is difficult. However, recent studies have shown a significant relationship between tax and expenditure structure of state and local governments and economic performance.[7]

State and local governments also employ a wide range of business location incentives. Incentives range from conventional investment tax credits, with the primary purpose of lowering the costs of purchasing or constructing new plants and equipment, to property tax abatement programs which partially or totally forgive tax liability on eligible property. Implementation, eligibility requirements, and subsidy size vary considerably across states, yielding differential effects.

Whether government spending can be classified as a "shock" depends on the speed and magnitude of the change in the size and composition of government expenditures and taxes. Tracking the change in state and local government expenditures during the last three decades reveals that the size of the local public sector has changed, and in some states the change has been significant. For instance, Louisiana's and West Virginia's government share of GSP increased at an annual rate of greater than 1.0 percent between 1965 and 1986. South Dakota's and New Hampshire's share shrunk by more than 1.0 percent during the same period. The composition of state and local government expenditure has also changed significantly over the same time period. Most striking is

Table 3.3
Shares of State GSP by Various State and Local Government Expenditure Categories, Averaged Over 1964-1986

State	Total	Capital outlays	Education	Fire & police	Social services
Alabama	0.169	0.036	0.065	0.006	0.017
Alaska	0.226	0.078	0.067	0.006	0.009
Arizona	0.170	0.048	0.075	0.010	0.008
Arkansas	0.144	0.031	0.056	0.004	0.017
California	0.163	0.027	0.057	0.009	0.025
Colorado	0.157	0.034	0.068	0.007	0.015
Connecticut	0.133	0.023	0.047	0.007	0.015
Delaware	0.167	0.038	0.069	0.006	0.012
Florida	0.151	0.035	0.056	0.009	0.009
Georgia	0.155	0.035	0.057	0.006	0.015
Hawaii	0.219	0.052	0.066	0.010	0.020
Idaho	0.157	0.033	0.060	0.006	0.012
Illinois	0.127	0.023	0.048	0.007	0.016
Indiana	0.122	0.022	0.057	0.005	0.009
Iowa	0.154	0.030	0.066	0.005	0.014
Kansas	0.138	0.029	0.057	0.005	0.012
Kentucky	0.141	0.033	0.053	0.005	0.016
Louisiana	0.105	0.022	0.036	0.004	0.011
Maine	0.176	0.029	0.064	0.007	0.024
Maryland	0.190	0.041	0.073	0.010	0.017
Massachusetts	0.163	0.025	0.052	0.011	0.027
Michigan	0.158	0.024	0.064	0.008	0.021

Minnesota	0.174	0.035	0.069	0.005	0.021
Mississippi	0.174	0.036	0.064	0.005	0.018
Missouri	0.126	0.025	0.049	0.007	0.013
Montana	0.169	0.040	0.067	0.005	0.012
Nebraska	0.147	0.048	0.061	0.005	0.011
Nevada	0.154	0.038	0.047	0.011	0.008
New Hampshire	0.150	0.030	0.055	0.007	0.015
New Jersey	0.143	0.021	0.052	0.009	0.015
New Mexico	0.153	0.031	0.068	0.006	0.012
New York	0.192	0.030	0.060	0.011	0.028
North Carolina	0.137	0.027	0.060	0.006	0.012
North Dakota	0.170	0.037	0.099	0.004	0.012
Ohio	0.128	0.024	0.050	0.006	0.014
Oklahoma	0.126	0.025	0.049	0.005	0.018
Oregon	0.181	0.034	0.073	0.009	0.014
Pennsylvania	0.144	0.025	0.054	0.006	0.020
Rhode Island	0.185	0.026	0.064	0.010	0.029
South Carolina	0.166	0.034	0.072	0.006	0.012
South Dakota	0.188	0.045	0.076	0.005	0.015
Tennessee	0.146	0.037	0.053	0.006	0.013
Texas	0.099	0.025	0.042	0.004	0.008
Utah	0.176	0.048	0.086	0.006	0.013
Vermont	0.192	0.035	0.073	0.005	0.022
Virginia	0.159	0.034	0.065	0.007	0.012
Washington	0.171	0.052	0.069	0.007	0.016
West Virginia	0.150	0.032	0.061	0.004	0.013
Wisconsin	0.172	0.029	0.070	0.008	0.021
Wyoming	0.116	0.033	0.054	0.005	0.006

SOURCES: U.S. Department of Commerce, Bureau of Economic Analysis for GSP estimates and Census Bureau for state government expenditures.

the uniform decline in capital outlays relative to GSP by all states, except Wyoming, and the increase in social services (table 3.3).[8]

Tax structure has also changed. The most dramatic change has been a sharp decline in property taxes as a revenue source, particularly in states such as California and Massachusetts, which passed property tax limitation measures during the late 1970s and early 1980s. The fallout from the passage of these messages changed not only the tax structure within these states but also the level of funding available for various government services. For example, as property tax revenues dwindled in California, local school districts were forced to turn to the state government for funding. This reliance on state funds reduced local school district autonomy, which in turn reduced the variation in school expenditures across California school districts. More recently, Oregon's passage of a property tax limitation forced the state to contribute a larger share to local schools, which diverted funds from various state agencies, such as higher education.

In summary, shocks come from many sources. Some are generated from within a region, while others originate from outside. Except for the most severe and pervasive shocks, such as sudden oil price changes, it is difficult to point to any one jolt as the specific event that significantly pushed a local labor market off its historical course. Rather, series of disturbances continuously shift labor supply and demand, and periodically an accumulation of the shocks yields perceptible effects on local markets.

Wages in Local Labor Markets

Sluggish Wage Adjustment

Wages are determined by explicit or implicit labor contracts. As a result, wages may take time to adjust. Explicit contracts are most prevalent in the unionized sectors. These contracts are usually three years in length. Except for the relatively few contracts with cost-of-living adjustments (COLAs), nominal wages are generally fixed throughout the duration of the agreement, or increase according to predetermined increments not contingent on current economic conditions. Although unions account for only 18 percent of the workforce, their indirect influence on related, but nonunion, sectors extends their influence considerably further.

Implicit contracts are not necessarily contractually binding for individual workers, as with union contracts or other formal agreements. However, since the cost of evaluating employees and altering relative wage structures is quite costly for businesses, wages within and across sectors do not change that frequently.

Further support for the slow adjustment of wages comes from evidence that employers are not price-takers in the labor markets but have the ability, within bounds, to set wages. Groshen (1991) documents significant and persistant wage dispersion among individual employers. She offers four explanations of how employers can systematically offer different wages.

The first suggests that employers systematically sort workers by ability. Consequently, the employer offering the highest wages would employ the most productive workers. Second, wages vary because of compensation for different working conditions. Workers may be compensated with high wages for little job security, poor working conditions, or few fringe benefits. Third, firms may be able to afford wage payments above the market rate because of savings on worker supervision, turnover, or other factors. In addition, some companies count on the fact that workers who know they are being paid above market rate are less likely to quit, or risk losing their job through shirking or carelessness. Fourth, employees are sometimes able to claim a share of the profits generated by firms in imperfectly competitive markets. Therefore, wages are not disciplined solely by market conditions, leaving employers with discretion in setting the level of compensation and in the timing by which wages change.

Evidence of Sluggish Wage Adjustment

Considerable attention has been given to exploring wage responses to demand changes. Many studies have examined whether nominal and real aggregate wages are responsive to aggregate demand changes, as reflected in national business cycles. A survey of these studies by Kniesner and Goldsmith (1987) finds conflicting results during the postwar period in which real wages are procyclical, countercyclical, and acyclical. They point out that the wide range of findings result in part from different sample periods examined and compositional changes in the employment over a business cycle. More recent research on the cyclical behavior of real wages has used individual data. The basic conclusion emerging from these studies is that real wages are not responsive to business cycle fluctuations.

In terms of understanding the market adjustment process, perhaps a more relevant issue is the relative variability among wages and employment. If wages are less sensitive than employment to demand changes, then much of the market adjustment may come through employment. One of the more recent and most comprehensive examinations of this issue is a study by Holzer and Montgomery (1990). They use data from individual firms representing all two-digit industries to estimate the adjustment of wages and employment to shifts in demand. Their findings support the notion that nominal wages adjust slowly and are rigid downward. Furthermore, they find that firms primarily adjust employment levels rather than wage levels in response to demand changes. They estimate that the variation in employment is 30 times greater than the variation in wages.

Other studies based on aggregate analysis support the rigidity of nominal wages. For example, Brown (1982) estimates that it takes manufacturing wages upwards of seven years to return to an equilibrium steady state after experiencing a shock. Groshen (1991), looking at the wage-setting behavior of individual companies, provides strong evidence that wages are remarkably persistent across establishments. Tracking wages offered by the same establishments over a 33-year period, she finds that it is highly likely that companies paying high wages at the beginning of the period are still paying high wages today.

The sensitivity of wage adjustments to institutional and industrial composition has also been addressed by Holzer and Montgomery. However, while they find supporting evidence of rigid wages, these factors exhibit little effect on wage adjustment. In particular, they find that the downward rigidity in wages is no more pronounced in unionized firms than in nonunionized firms. Furthermore, downward wage rigidity is not significantly different in large firms, manufacturing, or highly skilled industries. Based on these estimates, there is no apparent reason for regional differences in wage adjustments resulting from regional differences in union representation or in industry mix. We reexamine this issue in chapter 5 and concur with their results for wages, but find differences in employment responses between union and nonunion firms.

Regional Wage Differentials

One would expect that, given the highly integrated regional economies within the United States, regional wage differentials would be minimal, if not nonexistent. Goods, services, labor, and capital flow freely across state boundaries. A common language, generally a common culture, a common currency, and a federal system of government contribute to what one believes to be a well-greased regional adjustment process. Nonetheless, significant regional wage differentials do exist.[9]

Such differentials are difficult to explain within a neoclassical framework in which regions and factors of production are identical and all potentially mobile factors are free to move in response to interregional factor price differentials. In fact, under special conditions, regional wages would be the same even if workers were immobile, as long as other factors of production flowed freely among regions or if goods flowed unimpaired. However, it is unlikely that these special conditions are met. If regional differences exist in technology, taxes, market share, agglomeration economies, and unions, the special conditions are violated and regional wage differentials would emerge.

Another reason for regional wage differentials is that some factors affecting wages are immobile. For instance, each region has geographic and climatic characteristics unique to that area. Even for those areas that share common features, the quality and quantity of site-specific characteristics may differ. Therefore, firms or households may be willing to pay or accept different levels of wages depending upon the value they place on these attributes.

One often-cited reason for high wages is the high housing prices that individuals face in some regions of the country, most notably Los Angeles, San Francisco, and New York. However, to think that high wages only compensate for high rents is erroneous. Rents are high in areas for the same reason that wages might be expected to be low in those same areas—site-specific attributes. For example, Southern California is attractive for several reasons, and one of the most frequently mentioned is the mild climate. Climate is definitely an attribute that cannot be transported to a place like Cleveland. Those who prefer Southern California's climate to Cleveland's bid up the price of land in Southern California and at the same time are willing to accept relatively lower wages to live there. In this case wages and rents are inversely related.

A mild climate may also give firms an advantage by lowering their costs of heating buildings and protecting processes and inventory from colder weather. Firms then are able to pay higher labor costs in milder climates and still compete with firms elsewhere. The correlation between wages and rents depends upon which effect dominates. The relationship between wages and rents results from the confluence of the effects of climate and other immobile factors, and not from compensation for higher rents. Therefore, it is appropriate to consider nominal wage differentials when discussing the market adjustment process, without taking into account housing costs.[10]

This discussion highlights the distinction between long-run wage differentials and slow wage adjustment. To explain why wage rates differ across regions, even in a steady state situation, site-specific attributes are central. To understand why regional wages do not necessarily return quickly to their long-run relationship with the national average, impediments to mobility and trade are the appropriate explanation.

Nominal wages vary considerably across metropolitan areas. Using individual wage data from the 1988 *Current Population Survey* (CPS), the gap between the metropolitan areas with the highest and lowest average wage is 36 percentage points, as shown in column 1 of table 3.4. San Francisco topped the list of the 44 metropolitan areas listed in the CPS, with an average wage of 28.3 percent above the national average. At the other extreme was Tampa–St. Petersburg with a wage of 7.8 percent below the national average.

These differentials are not simply the result of regional variations in worker characteristics. We standardized the regional wage for each metropolitan area by taking into account the effects of worker characteristics (and other attributes not specific to the metropolitan area). By netting out the effects of these characteristics on a worker's wage,

Table 3.4
1988 Metropolitan Wage Differentials
(percentage difference from national average)

Rank	Metropolitan area	Actual	Skill-adjusted
1	San Francisco	28.3	21.3
2	San Jose	32.7	20.2
3	Nassau-Suffolk	25.4	18.7
4	Paterson, NJ	22.8	16.6
5	New York	21.3	16.1
6	Newark	19.8	15.7
7	Boston	20.7	14.9
8	Washington, DC	21.6	14.0
9	Minneapolis-St. Paul	14.0	12.8
10	Anaheim	14.0	12.7
11	Seattle-Everett	16.4	11.9
12	San Bernardino	12.7	10.9
13	Sacramento	15.6	10.4
14	Detroit	11.0	10.3
15	Los Angeles	10.8	10.1
16	Chicago	11.3	9.7
17	Philadelphia	11.6	8.9
18	San Diego	11.8	8.9
19	Gary-Hammond	8.5	7.4
20	Dallas	7.9	6.1
21	Atlanta	9.4	6.1
22	Denver	10.7	5.2
23	Baltimore	8.6	5.1
24	Kansas City	8.6	3.9
25	Rochester	9.1	3.6
26	Portland	5.1	3.6
27	Cleveland	5.3	3.3
28	St. Louis	2.9	3.0
29	Columbus, OH	5.1	1.8
30	Houston	4.7	1.7
31	Cincinnati	3.6	1.6
32	Fort Worth	5.0	1.2
33	Milwaukee	2.7	0.7
34	Albany	−1.7	−0.4
35	Miami	−4.2	−0.9
36	Akron	0.3	−1.4
37	Greensboro	−3.8	−2.0
38	Indianapolis	−2.2	−2.3
39	Pittsburgh	0.0	−2.8
40	Buffalo	−5.1	−3.5
41	New Orleans	−4.3	−4.0
42	Norfolk-Portsmouth	−12.8	−6.7
43	Birmingham	−5.8	−7.7
44	Tampa-St. Petersburg	−7.8	−8.8

NOTE: Wage differentials are derived from *Current Population Survey* files, using the technique described in the text.

we, in effect, record what an identical worker would earn in each of the various metropolitan labor markets.

The second column of table 3.4 lists these adjusted wages relative to the national average. Although the adjusted differentials are generally smaller than the differentials based on actual wages, it is still obvious that regional wages vary significantly. Therefore, regional wage differentials are not simply the result of different regional compositions of the workforce in terms of occupation, industry, age, educational attainment, and union representation, but the value that regional labor markets place on workers' attributes.

Variations in wages across regions have increased since 1980, after converging for almost half a century. For nine census regions between 1973 and 1987, this divergence can be attributed primarily to differences in the value individual regional labor markets place on worker attributes. In particular, regional labor markets value worker skills differently, as measured by a worker's occupation, even after controlling for a worker's industry of employment. At the same time, the composition of regional workforces has looked increasingly alike.[11] Nevertheless, the growing similarity of regional workers is not enough to offset the growing disparity in compensation of these employees. Increased regional differences in returns to worker attributes coincide with several episodes in which areas were hit disproportionately by shocks. Three instances come to mind: a general increase in foreign competition, the collapse of oil prices in the early 1980s, and the severe back-to-back recessions of 1980–82.

These factors struck some regions harder than others, producing different patterns of change in regional wage differentials. The West South Central states of Texas and Louisiana were particularly hurt when the bottom dropped out of oil prices. This downturn thwarted the sizable gains achieved by that region in previous years in narrowing its wage gap.

The farming states of the West North Central region were also severely affected by the recession and the ensuing farm crisis of the early 1980s. After converging toward the national average throughout the 1970s, wages in that region diverged significantly, falling from 7.0 percent below the national average at the beginning of the 1980s to 10.9 percent below the average toward the end of the decade. Wages in other regions continued to grow faster than the national average in spite of the recession. For example, the Pacific region, especially California, was only mildly affected, with its regional wage differential expanding by a percentage point between 1979–81 and 1985–87.

Factors other than the three economic shocks listed above may also have contributed to the wage divergence. Another possibility is state tax policy. The late 1970s and early 1980s saw the phaseout of substantial federal grant programs to states and municipalities. Many of these programs were designed to help equalize the fiscal burden across regions. As these funds dried up, a number of state and local governments found it necessary to raise tax rates to fund the existing programs, while others decided to cut or scale back programs. These different responses could lead to an increase in regional differences in tax rates, which in turn could affect the location of firms and ultimately the demand for labor.

Persistence of Regional Wage Differentials

How persistent are regional wage differentials? Although we pursue this question more rigorously in chapter 4, it is instructive to note at this point the tendency for the ranking of metropolitan wage differentials to remain relatively constant over time. To calculate the persistence of regional wage differentials, we measured the rank-order correlation of metropolitan wage differentials (relative to the United States) in the current year and with each successive year. This process is repeated by computing the correlation of the wage differential in the current year with the wage differential two years later, then three years later, and so forth.

Figure 3.1 illustrates the relative consistency of the rank-ordering of metropolitan wages over time. The correlation between any two adjacent years averages to 0.90. The correlation remains relatively high even for the longer time spans. For a span of five years, the correlation has decayed only 0.10 percentage points to around 0.80. For a span of 10 years, the correlation coefficient is 0.70. This relatively moderate decay of the correlation coefficients indicates that metropolitan areas for the most part preserve their wage-differential ranking. These results

Figure 3.1
Persistence of Metropolitan Wage and Unemployment Differentials

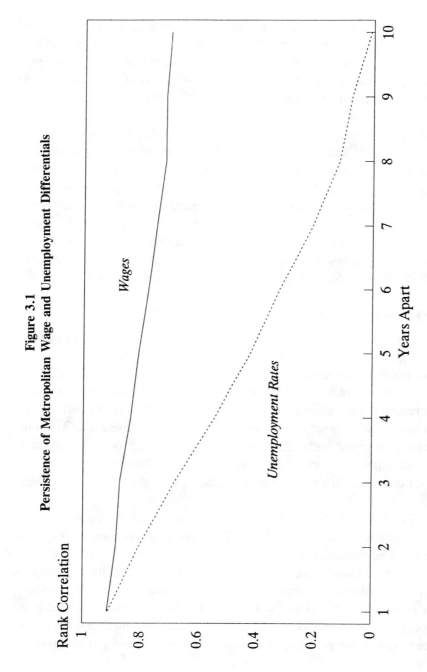

SOURCE: Current Population Survey.

support at the regional level the notion that wages do not adjust instantaneously to one-time shocks. The findings are also consistent with cities adjusting instantly to a series of disturbances, in which these shocks gradually change the ranking of cities according to wages.

Employment and Unemployment in Local Labor Markets

Employment Adjustments

According to Holzer and Montgomery (1990), businesses are considerably more likely to change employment than to change wages in response to shocks. Even so, in the aggregate, the stickiness of wages has contributed in part to a degree of persistence among unemployment rates. While unemployment rates are definitely countercyclical, we have also seen a general upward trend in these rates over the last two decades. Murphy and Topel (1987) provide a comprehensive look at the increase in aggregate unemployment and offer, along with several other key findings, the observation that the mobility of workers across industries has declined, and that both employed and unemployed individuals are less likely to move between industries in periods of high unemployment. Furthermore, they report that much of the increase in unemployment is accounted for by individuals who do not change industries.

The decline in worker mobility across industries opens up the possibility that demand shocks that hit one sector harder than another (or may even benefit one sector to the detriment of another) could lead to an increase in unemployment. Lilien (1982) developed this theory based on the assumption that labor is attached to specific labor market sectors. Under this assumption, the initial effect of a shift in demand between sectors is to decrease employment in the declining sector, thus increasing unemployment there, and to increase employment (decrease unemployment) in the expanding sector. If workers were perfectly mobile, shifts in the sectoral composition of demand for labor would not alter the aggregate level of demand for labor. Employment losses in contracting firms would be exactly matched by employment gains in expanding firms. However, if workers are not perfectly mobile, as

Lilien contends, then shifts in employment demand can lead to temporary increases in unemployment.

This theory has met with some opposition. Abraham and Katz (1986) demonstrate that in an economy in which sectors have different cyclical sensitivities, aggregate demand movements could lead to the same dispersion across sectors predicted by Lilien. In addition, Evans (1986) generates sectoral unemployment by assuming that wages have different degrees of rigidity across sectors. In this case, failure of wages to fall in sectors with declining demand causes unemployment. In expanding sectors, wages rise so that there is no offsetting decline in unemployment.

Since regions possess different industrial compositions, one would expect that unemployment rates would vary considerably across regional economies. On the other hand, these economies are thought to be closely linked with labor moving freely throughout, which would reduce the regional unemployment rate differentials. The question is an empirical one.

Regional Unemployment Differentials

There is considerable literature, starting with Hall (1970), suggesting that local unemployment differentials persist. Unemployment rates differ markedly among the sample of large metropolitan areas listed in table 3.5. Between 1975 and 1986, unemployment rates ranged from a high of 16.0 percent during the depths of the 1980–82 recession to a low of 3.1 percent during the economic expansion of the late 1970s. However, even during the severe recession in 1982, some metropolitan areas experienced unemployment rates as low as 5.7 percent. The range of unemployment rates among these metropolitan areas in any one year varied from a high of 10.6 percentage points in 1984 to a low of 5.4 percentage points in 1978. Somewhat surprisingly, both the greatest and lowest spreads occurred during economic expansions, which suggests that the dispersion of unemployment rates is acyclical.[12]

How persistent are these metropolitan unemployment rates over time? Using the same methodology as for wages, we find considerably less persistence of unemployment rates than we found for wages. Although the consecutive-year correlations are similar to the wage correlations,

Table 3.5
Metropolitan Unemployment Rates for Selected Years

Metropolitan area	Unemployment Rates			
	1980	1981	1982	1986
Akron	8.60	9.58	11.81	8.01
Albany	5.89	6.17	7.00	5.08
Anaheim	4.30	4.67	7.22	3.99
Atlanta	5.48	5.46	6.43	4.54
Baltimore	7.51	8.39	9.88	5.15
Birmingham	9.04	10.68	13.89	8.23
Boston	5.27	6.00	7.20	3.53
Buffalo	9.74	9.53	12.69	7.52
Chicago	7.73	8.17	10.61	7.21
Cincinnati	7.01	8.71	10.50	6.49
Cleveland	7.25	8.54	10.73	7.51
Columbus	5.65	7.70	8.99	5.92
Dallas	4.48	4.67	5.68	5.96
Denver	5.17	4.88	6.57	6.55
Detroit	13.13	13.04	15.98	8.17
Gary	11.18	11.64	15.66	11.68
Greensboro	5.92	5.71	8.23	4.63
Houston	3.98	4.13	6.47	10.30
Indianapolis	7.24	8.31	9.38	5.12
Kansas City	6.41	6.62	7.84	4.63
Los Angeles	6.58	6.90	9.30	6.66
Miami	8.15	9.49	10.09	6.68
Milwaukee	6.24	7.40	10.53	6.11
Minneapolis	4.48	4.45	6.42	4.18
Nassau–Suffolk	5.92	5.90	6.35	4.34
New Orleans	5.91	7.77	9.31	10.79
New York	7.68	7.97	8.61	6.43
Newark	7.12	7.14	8.68	5.12
Norfolk	5.46	6.34	7.24	4.87
Paterson, NJ	9.13	8.78	11.04	6.04
Philadelphia	6.82	7.53	8.63	5.20
Pittsburgh	7.18	7.46	12.29	8.07
Portland, OR	6.30	7.93	10.10	7.39
Riverside	7.62	8.39	12.18	6.40
Rochester	5.96	5.86	7.23	5.68
Sacramento	7.99	8.91	11.39	6.24
St. Louis	8.02	8.44	9.87	6.98
San Diego	6.81	6.88	9.25	4.98
San Francisco	5.58	6.12	8.20	5.24
San Jose	5.09	5.93	7.52	5.78
Seattle	6.35	7.77	10.28	6.50
Tampa	5.12	5.76	7.27	5.05
Washington, DC	4.06	4.90	5.76	3.50

SOURCE: U.S. Bureau of Labor Statistics.

the correlations for unemployment rates quickly decay for years farther apart, as shown in figure 3.1. For example, over a span of five
years, the correlation drops to 0.40, half the value of the consecutive-
year correlation. For a span of 10 years, the correlation approaches
zero. Therefore, it appears that the ranking of metropolitan areas according to unemployment rates changes appreciably over time.

The implication is that over time the fortune of a metropolitan area
changes. During one period, unemployment rates may be relatively low,
while during another period, they may be relatively high. The fact that
the location of depressed regions varies over time further suggests that
regional unemployment rates appear to be only weakly related to one
another. Therefore, it is reasonable to conclude that conditions within
local labor markets are shaped primarily by internal conditions. This
position finds support in recent empirical research examining turnover
and gross employment flows. Dunne, Roberts, and Samuelson (1989),
for example, find that the vast majority of employment turnover occurs across plants within the same industry and geographic region.

Following Cleveland's and San Diego's ranking over the 12-year
period illustrates this point, as shown in figure 3.2. During the latter
half of the 1970s, Cleveland's unemployment rate consistently dropped, bottoming out in 1978 at thirty-fifth among the 43 largest
metropolitan areas. Since then, the unemployment rate relative to other
metropolitan areas has steadily increased until throughout the 1980s it
was among the 10 highest. San Diego also changed its ranking appreciably during the 12-year period, but in a direction opposite to the
ranking of Cleveland. Starting in the 1970s, San Diego was among the
10 metropolitan areas with the highest unemployment rates. However,
from that point on, rates fell consistently until San Diego ranked among
the 10 areas with the lowest unemployment rates.

In contrast, wage-rate ranking for these two areas remained relatively constant throughout the period, as shown in figure 3.3. Wage levels
in both Cleveland and San Diego fluctuated around the middle of the
sample group. This relatively constant ranking is consistent with the
persistence in wage rates as measured by the various correlations described above.

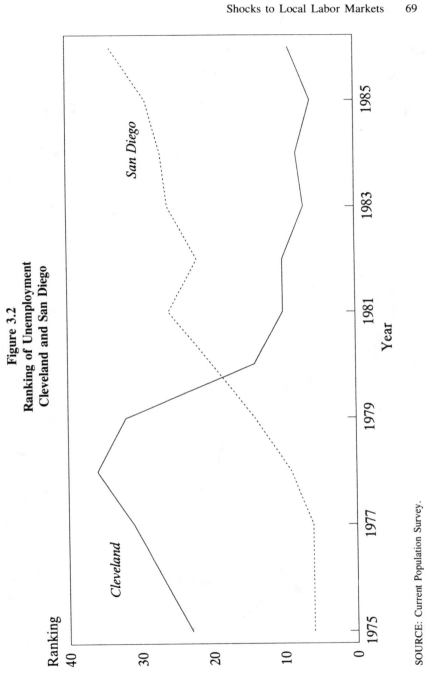

Figure 3.2
Ranking of Unemployment
Cleveland and San Diego

SOURCE: Current Population Survey.

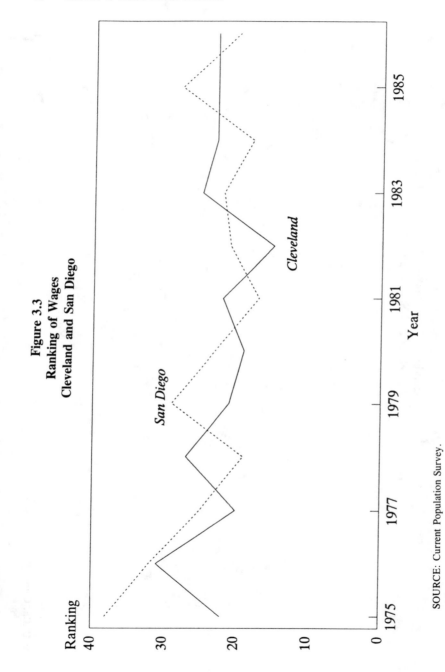

Figure 3.3
Ranking of Wages
Cleveland and San Diego

SOURCE: Current Population Survey.

Evidence from metropolitan economies is consistent with findings from micro-level data that wages are much less flexible than employment. Consequently, much of the regional adjustment to shocks would be expected to come through adjustments in employment components rather than wages. Several studies have examined the relationship between regional wages and unemployment. Two are discussed in the next section.

Relationship Between Regional Wages and Unemployment

Several studies have estimated the relationship between wages and short-run and long-run unemployment. For example, Adams (1985), using wages of individual workers over time, finds wage premiums for longer-run trends in state unemployment. He also finds a negative correlation between wages and shorter-run current unemployment rates of industries. Negative short-run shocks to industries generate wage cuts, while positive shocks generate wage hikes. Consequently, while workers are compensated for living in local labor markets that have permanently higher unemployment rates, wages in local labor markets facilitate adjustment to temporary shocks.

Marston (1985) implicitly challenges the short-run adjustment process by questioning whether wages are flexible enough to bring local labor markets back to equilibrium after an employment shock. He cites institutional constraints, such as explicit and implicit labor contracts, as contributing to the rigidity of wages. He points out that if firms tend to smooth out fluctuations in the wages they pay, then demand shocks will tend to affect unemployment more than wages—a result consistent with Holzer and Montgomery's (1990) analysis at the firm level.

On the other hand, if firms adjust wages to reflect changing short-run market conditions, then wages will change more than unemployment. Both of these scenarios assume that the cost of mobility is sufficiently high so that workers do not migrate between regions immediately in response to employment demand shocks. Consequently, the short-run adjustment process must entail a change in either wages or unemployment, or both. Similar to Adams, Marston also allows for the possibility that in equilibrium, individuals residing in areas of higher permanent unemployment will be compensated by higher wages.

Because Marston assumes that unemployment rates adjust more than wages in the event of a demand shock to a local labor market, he takes an empirical approach counter to Adams's. Instead of explaining regional wage differentials by differences in unemployment rates, he explains regional differences in unemployment rates by regional differences in wages. In the same way as Adams, Marston controls for other factors, including state unemployment insurance wage-replacement rates.

Marston's estimates, based on 30 metropolitan areas during the 1970s, strongly support the equilibrium view—wages and unemployment rates are positively correlated. In addition, unemployment differentials created by shocks are smaller on average than the unemployment rate differentials compensated by other factors. Furthermore, Marston finds that differential regional unemployment rates induced by shocks tend to be eliminated by worker mobility within a year.

Marston explains this quick response with two facts. First, the movement toward equilibrium merely requires that a small part of the labor force be mobile. On the surface, this requirement seems to fly in the face of recent observations on the immobility of displaced workers. For instance, Flaim and Sehgal (1985), in a survey of displaced workers, observe that only a small percentage of workers who lost their jobs moved to a different city or county in search of work. However, Marston's point is that so long as some workers are mobile, equilibrium will be achieved. Nonetheless, the group of workers who are the least mobile will feel the greatest effects of the adjustment, while the most mobile group will be the least affected, by escaping the major consequences of the shock.

Second, Marston is convinced that enough migration occurs among areas within a short enough time span to smooth out the temporary differentials in unemployment rates across metropolitan labor markets. Marston argues that migration is sufficient to equilibrate markets if the flow of people moving between areas in a given time span is large compared with the disequilibrium component of the local labor market's unemployment rate. Marston calculates this component to be 0.8 percent of the labor force for his sample of metropolitan areas, which is one-quarter the size of the percentage of the population that moves to new metropolitan areas each year.

Conclusion

There appears to be sufficient evidence that regions are affected by shocks of different types and magnitudes, and that these effects vary over time and across regions. Wages and employment do not adjust instantaneously to shocks, but employment appears to adjust faster than wages to changes in labor market conditions. Wage differentials, in particular, exhibit a high degree of persistence, with a rank correlation of roughly 0.80 at points a decade apart.

Despite the general sluggishness, local labor markets have a tendency to move toward equilibrium. In the short run, high unemployment rates tend to push wages down, while tight labor markets push wages up. In the long run, however, areas with chronically high unemployment also have high wages, which some have interpreted as compensating workers for poor employment opportunities.

NOTES

1. See *Ohio's Third Century, Meeting the Economic Challenge Through Science and Technology,* A Report of the Ohio Science and Technology Commission.

2. The estimates come from Hulten and Schwab (1991), which is an extension of Hulten and Schwab (1984).

3. These estimates are taken from Eberts (1990a).

4. Eberts (1990b) describes the differences in magnitude and timing between state and national business cycles.

5. For an analysis of the effect of military spending on regional growth, see Markusen (1988).

6. See Eberts (1991) for some empirical evidence on the linkage between public infrastructure and local economic development.

7. See Mofidi and Stone (1990) for a discussion of these relationships.

8. For more discussion of these trends, see Eberts and Gronberg (1991).

9. For example, see Beeson and Eberts (1987), Gerking and Weirick (1983), and Sahling and Smith (1983).

10. For more detailed discussion of these relationships, see Beeson and Eberts (1987).

11. Eberts (1989) analyzes the determinants of the recent divergence in regional wages and shows that it results primarily from regional labor markets valuing worker attributes differently.

12. Barry Eichengreen, "Currency Union," *Economic Policy* (April 1986) finds the same behavior using U.S. census regions for the period 1960 to 1988.

4

Estimates of Local
Labor Market Adjustment

In previous chapters, we have brought together evidence that wage and employment changes are sufficiently sluggish that local labor markets do not adjust quickly to shocks. In this chapter, we present a more integrated approach to address fundamental questions about the dynamics of local labor markets. How elastic are demand and supply curves for labor in major metropolitan labor markets? How long does it take for wages and employment to respond to supply and demand shocks? What is the pattern of adjustment and does it differ for supply and demand shocks? How important are interactions between sectors in explaining the observed sluggishness?

To investigate these questions, we begin with a discussion of the major empirical issues, including the questions of how to identify demand and supply behavior in the observed data and how to control for the influence of other relevant factors on the local labor market. Next, we present estimates of labor demand and supply in a "representative" metropolitan area and demonstrate the dynamic response of local labor markets to both demand and supply shocks. We wish to avoid placing undue emphasis on the specific values of these estimates and the simulations based upon them. Instead, we rely upon them to provide useful insights into the patterns of adjustment in local labor markets. Finally, we examine the goods-producing and service-producing subsectors of local labor markets, as well as the interactions between the two sectors, and estimate the effect of changes in personal income on local labor market composition.

Empirical Specifications

Identifying Labor Demand and Supply

Our approach to identifying the separate demand and supply behavior in local labor markets is to exploit what we believe to be a recursive dynamic structure. Put simply, we assume that on the demand side employers first respond to a shock by changing employment rather than wages, so that employment is appropriately specified in a demand equation as a function of exogenous shocks and lagged wages. This recursive structure is consistent with studies by Topel (1986) and Holzer and Montgomery (1990). On the supply side, we assume that workers offer their labor via a reservation wage equation, so that wages are appropriately specified as a function of exogenous shocks and lagged employment.

Under classical assumptions regarding the error term in each equation, this recursive structure is sufficient to identify both labor demand and labor supply. Haynes and Stone (1985) demonstrate this approach to identification and offer several illustrations of its usefulness, including the vexing issue of aggregate supply (as it relates to the Phillips curve tradeoff between wage changes and unemployment) and demand relationships between unemployment and inflation.

To use this recursive structure, one must choose an interval between observations of market behavior that is short enough to afford the market under consideration contemporaneous effects between quantity (employment) and price (wage) when compared to the lagged effects. For labor markets, which are relatively sluggish, the interval of a year seems appropriate. In fact, we find little evidence of strong contemporaneous linkages between wages and employment in auxiliary estimates. For other markets that have inherently quicker price and quantity movements, quarterly or even hourly intervals might be more appropriate.

One possible objection to this approach is that it suppresses the influence of future anticipated shocks. Topel (1986), in particular, emphasizes the possible significance of future anticipated demand shocks on current labor supply, suggesting that households migrate between local labor markets years in advance of these shocks. We reject this approach as unrealistic, for the various reasons revealed in the previous two chapters. Instead, we assume that the transaction costs of migration are sufficiently high, and shocks (more than a year away) are sufficiently unanticipated to ensure that households do not move in advance of the disturbances. We do not believe that this assumption is heroic. Analyzing capital flows and interest rate differentials between the United States and Canada, Haynes (1988) demonstrates that the recursive approach has identifying power even for capital markets, which are relatively "frictionless" and dominated by highly informed agents.

Other Variables

We employ several methods for dealing with the problem of controlling for other influences on labor demand and supply. First, we follow the practice used by others of expressing the employment variables relative to the overall national trends. The metropolitan wage differentials are already expressed in relative form. This specification offers an implicit method of controlling for those influences common to all local labor markets, including aggregate business cycles, the (assumed) nationally uniform rental price of capital, prices of goods marketed in national markets, and the like. Second, by using first-differences of the dependent and independent variables, we are able to employ a fixed-effects model to control for city-specific variables that are fixed over time. The first-difference specification has the additional advantage of attenuating first-order autocorrelation, as evidenced by tests on the residuals.

In addition, we control for other influences on labor demand and supply by including binary dummy variables for each year in the regression data and, where jointly significant, binary dummy variables for each metropolitan area. One dummy variable in each case is omitted to avoid perfect multicollinearity. Inclusion of metropolitan dummy variables controls for metropolitan-specific intercept effects on the first-difference of each dependent variable. Because we have no direct interest in the coefficients on the year and metropolitan dummy variables, they are omitted from the tables in the interest of brevity.

Other Specification Issues

Rather than impose arbitrary restrictions on the pattern of the lag structure of each equation (e.g., by using one of a variety of coefficient "smoothing" techniques), we impose no restrictions on the dynamic structure other than truncating the length of each lag through experimentation, where the length of lag is specified generously. We do not expect, however, to be able to fully capture extremely long-term behavior, for example, gradual disinvestment in existing enterprises taking place over several decades. Thus, our estimates are best interpreted as relevant over the short to intermediate run for labor market behavior.

In addition, we follow the common practice of specifying the equations in multiplicative, double-logarithmic form, so that (after first-differencing and normalizing on the national average) the variables represent logarithmic rates of change relative to the national average. The logarithmic, first-difference specification leaves little evidence for concern regarding heteroscedasticity and first-order autocorrelation.

Estimates of Local
Labor Demand and Supply

Elasticities

Estimates of the wage coefficients in the labor demand equation and the employment coefficients in the labor supply equation are interpreted as the elasticities of labor demand and supply. As presented in table 4.1, the variables denoted by w and e represent the wage and employment variables, respectively, t refers to the contemporaneous time period, and the lag is indicated in parentheses beside each variable. Our emphasis in interpreting the estimates is on qualitative patterns and rough magnitudes of adjustment rather than on specific point estimates, which may vary to some extent with alternative specifications.

For labor demand, the wage coefficients are all significantly negative (at the 10 percent level) for lags out to six years. The wage elasticity of labor demand is -1.04, which is the cumulative response of the coefficient in the lagged wage variables. This estimate is significantly neg-

Table 4.1
Local Labor Demand and Supply Equation Estimates
(21 cities, *t*-statistics in parentheses)

Variable	Labor demand	Labor supply
intercept	0.012*	−0.017*
	(2.683)	(−1.938)
$w(t\text{-}1)$	−0.173**	
	(−1.917)	
$w(t\text{-}2)$	−0.156**	
	(−1.687)	
$w(t\text{-}3)$	−0.219***	
	(−2.888)	
$w(t\text{-}4)$	−0.151**	
	(2.093)	
$w(t\text{-}5)$	−0.263***	
	(−4.137)	
$w(t\text{-}6)$	−0.074*	
	(−1.324)	
$e(t\text{-}1)$		0.160**
		(2.234)
$e(t\text{-}2)$		−0.014
		(−0.190)
$e(t\text{-}3)$		0.005
		(0.070)
$e(t\text{-}4)$		0.237***
		(3.089)
$e(t\text{-}5)$		−0.149*
		(1.935)
$e(t\text{-}6)$		−0.033
		(−0.426)
R^2	0.506	0.176
Obs.	168	168

NOTES: The symbols * (**,***) denote statistical significance at the 10 (5, 1) percent level (one- or two-tailed test, as appropriate). Dependent variables are first-differences of the logarithms of employment and wages, respectively, relative to the national average. Metropolitan dummy variables are included in the demand equation; year dummy variables are included in both equations. See text for sources and details.

ative at the 1 percent level, yielding a strong negatively sloped demand curve. The equation includes metropolitan and year dummy variables, which enter significantly and contribute to the good fit of the equation (with an R^2 of 0.506).

For labor supply, the employment coefficients are significantly positive at lags 1 and 4 and significantly negative at lag 5. The cumulative response is 0.206, which is significantly positive at the 5 percent level. This cumulative value implies a wage elasticity of labor supply of 4.9, which is obtained by inverting to renormalize on employment. The fit of the equation (with an R^2 of 0.176) is substantially lower than that for labor demand, but still respectable for a first-difference specification. Year dummies are included in the equation, but city dummies are omitted because their coefficients were not statistically significant.

The fact that the distant lag coefficients on employment turn negative is expected and consistent with results in other markets examined by Haynes and Stone (1985). If one assumes that labor supply eventually becomes more elastic over time, then the employment coefficients in a supply-wage specification must eventually turn negative. Otherwise, supply will not be more elastic in the long run than in the short run. Of course, one expects the cumulative response to remain non-negative.

The overall pattern of the labor supply specification has an appealing, but not directly tested, interpretation. An initial increase in employment causes the supply wage to rise through the following year, and this rise appears sufficient to draw in additional workers without requiring further increases in the supply wage for the next two years. Presumably, these near-term expansions in the employed labor force are sustained primarily by current residents entering the labor force or by existing employees expanding their hours.

By the fourth year following an employment shock, however, a further rise in the supply wage is required, presumably because local expansion of the labor force is no longer sufficient. Yet, by the fifth year, and following significant increases in the supply wage during the previous four years, inmigration of new workers from other locales and continued expansion of the labor force from local residents are sufficient to mitigate, and partially reverse, previous increases in the supply wage. Of course, this scenario is speculative, but it is consistent with findings from previous chapters.

The demand and supply responses presented for local labor markets in table 4.1 are strikingly robust. Often, the debate regarding local labor market behavior is cast in terms of extremes. Many analysts and policymakers argue that local labor market responses are extremely weak and insufficient to provide a well-behaved, equilibrating labor market. Others argue that the labor market responses are so robust and quick that equilibrating adjustments are extremely rapid. As noted earlier, Topel (1986) and others argue that on the supply side households migrate years in advance of anticipated local demand shocks. The evidence in table 4.1 represents, in our view, a clear rejection of the first extreme view. Labor market responses in both demand and supply are quite strong. As we shall demonstrate below, the results also provide evidence suggesting that labor market adjustment is neither as rapid nor as smooth as implied by the alternative view.

Responses to a Permanent Demand Shock

To examine the response of a local labor market to a demand or supply shock, we can introduce an arbitrary shock to either the demand or supply equation and solve for the subsequent responses. Figure 4.1 presents the logarithmic response of wages and employment in a local labor market to an exogenous (positive) disturbance to labor demand. An innovation in the technology of production, an exogenous increase in the demand for the products produced in the local market, and an exogenous decrease in the price of other factors of production substitutable for labor are all examples of possible disturbances to labor demand. The disturbance is arbitrarily chosen to equal unity and occurs in year one, as represented in figure 4.1. Responses are plotted for 15 years—a period that appears sufficiently long for the system to converge to the new equilibrium.

Several characteristics of the response are particularly salient. First, in response to the demand shock, wages and employment move predominantly in the same direction—demand shocks tend to trace out supply, which has a positive (or at least non-negative slope). There is a slight tendency in some short subperiods of the adjustment for employment and wages to move in opposite directions. This occurs because initial changes in employment subsequently shift the supply curve,

Figure 4.1
Increase in Local Labor Demand

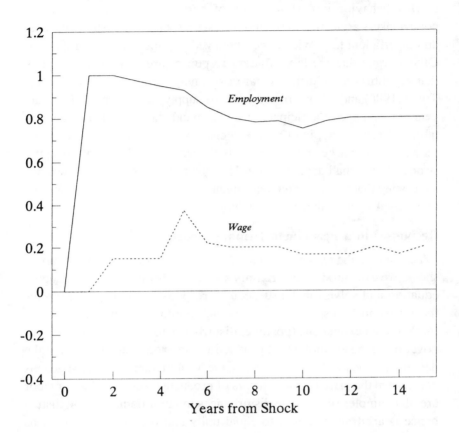

which then tends to trace out the inverse relationship between wages and employment in labor demand.

Second, the wage responses are delayed relative to the initial employment responses, consistent with our assumed recursive structure.[1] The lag between the peak in employment and the peak in the wage, for example, is four years. The wage response is also of smaller magnitude than the employment response, which is consistent with the findings from other studies reported in chapter 2. In our analysis, this divergence in magnitude occurs because the implied wage elasticity of labor supply is much greater than one in absolute value and because the simulated shock is to labor demand.

Third, both wages and employment "overshoot"—initially move beyond—their long-run equilibrium values in response to a disturbance to labor demand. The peak in employment is roughly 20 percent higher than the new equilibrium employment, and the peak in wages is almost double the new equilibrium wage. The overshooting phenomenon is familiar in models and estimates of asset markets with rapid speeds of adjustment, such as exchange rates, interest rates, and the like, but less familiar in models of relatively sluggish markets. The overshooting also occurs for both wages and employment, although the degree is proportionately greater for wages. Leonard (1987), in looking at ES202 data of individual firms in Wisconsin, found similar evidence of overshooting for employment.

Fourth, the full adjustment toward the new equilibrium clearly stretches out over a period in excess of a decade, indicating that the effects of a permanent shock to aggregate demand are felt in local labor markets for long periods. The adjustment period is particularly lengthy in relation to the typical tenure of local metropolitan government administrations. The long adjustment period is at odds with Marston's (1985) findings that labor markets, as measured by unemployment rates, return to equilibrium within a year. However, our results are consistent with work by Pissarides and McMaster (1990), who found a protracted adjustment process of up to 20 years for regional labor markets in Great Britain.

Responses to a Permanent Supply Shock

Figure 4.2 presents the response of a local labor market to a permanent (positive) shock to labor supply. An example of such a supply shock might be an exogenous inmigration of households attracted to a region because of its climate or familiar culture, or because of political uncertainties in other parts of the world. For example, Miami and Los Angeles have experienced a stream of new households during the last decade for these very reasons. In addition, a supply shock may also occur because of an exogenous change in local nonlabor income. Again, the magnitude of the shock is arbitrarily chosen to equal unity and occurs in year one. An increase in labor supply is expressed as a decline in supply wage.

There are two predictable differences between the responses to the demand shock in figure 4.1 and the responses to the supply shock in figure 4.2. First, a supply shock causes wages and employment to move predominantly in opposite directions—supply shocks tend to trace out the inverse demand relationship between wages and employment. Second, the employment response is delayed relative to the initial wage response, consistent with the recursive structure. The peak of employment, for example, occurs six years later than the peak (in absolute value) for the wage.

However, there are also a number of similarities. The employment and wage responses are roughly proportional in the new equilibrium. This similarity occurs because the wage elasticity of labor demand is roughly equal to one, and because the simulated shock is to labor supply. As before, the adjustment to a shock is spread over a period in excess of a decade, and both wages and employment overshoot their new equilibrium values. For employment, the overshooting is again about 20 percent greater than the new equilibrium value. For wages, however, the overshooting is now roughly similar to that for employment, about 20 percent of the new equilibrium value, rather than the almost 100 percent response to the demand shock depicted in figure 4.1.

Examination of the responses in figures 4.1 and 4.2 reveals very strong market responses in both demand and supply, but the system response is protracted over what appears to be at least 10 to 12 years. The

Figure 4.2
Increase in Local Labor Supply

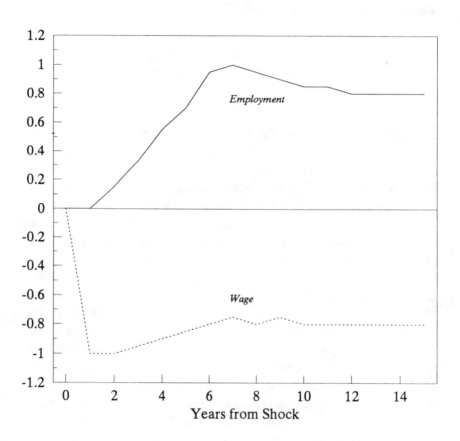

responses also appear to exhibit overshooting. We believe that these findings reject both extreme views of local labor markets: labor market adjustment is protracted but robust.

Sector Estimates of Local
Labor Demand and Supply

Elasticities

Local labor markets are far from being homogeneous in either demand or supply. Heterogeneity is important not only for explaining variations in labor markets from city to city, but also for understanding how the dynamic interactions among the various sectors of a local labor market contribute to the behavior of the market as a whole. As mentioned earlier, some researchers have attributed the slow adjustment to job reallocation across sectors within local labor markets. This section offers additional insight into this relationship.

As a first step in examining disaggregate behavior of local labor markets, we divide the local market into the goods-producing and service-producing sectors. As described in the data appendix, the goods-producing sector includes (1) construction and (2) manufacturing. The service-producing sector includes (1) transportation, communications, and public utilities, (2) wholesale and retail trade, (3) financial, insurance, and real estate, (4) services, and (5) government. Our approach is first to estimate a relatively simple specification for each sector and then introduce more comprehensive interactions between the sectors.

Table 4.2 presents estimates of labor demand and supply equations for the goods-producing and service-producing sectors. The equations are specified similarly to the aggregate specifications presented in table 4.1, except that the wage from the other sector is introduced as an alternative wage in each sector's labor supply equation. For example, in the demand equation for the goods sector, the service-sector wages are included in the equation along with the goods-sector wages. In addition, we add goods employment to service-sector demand to reflect spillover from the goods sector. The g and s prefixes refer, respectively, to the goods-producing and service-producing sectors. Lag lengths for

Table 4.2
Local Labor Demand and Supply Equations by Sector
(21 cities, *t*-statistics in parentheses)

Variable	Goods-producing sector		Service-producing sector	
	Demand	Supply	Demand	Supply
intercept	−0.035	0.009	−0.004	0.010*
	(−0.410)	(1.387)	(−0.359)	(1.783)
gw(*t*-1)	−0.127			0.050
	(−0.209)			(0.713)
gw(*t*-2)	−0.373			0.208***
	(−0.639)			(3.078)
gw(*t*-3)	−1.251***			0.048
	(−2.500)			(0.796)
ge(*t*-1)		0.015		
		(1.106)		
ge(*t*-2)		0.008		
		(0.507)		
ge(*t*-3)		−0.010		
		(−0.750)		
sw(*t*-1)		−0.047	−0.137	
		(−0.496)	(−1.282)	
sw(*t*-2)		0.085	−0.085	
		(1.061)	(−0.898)	
sw(*t*-3)		0.134**	−0.005	
		(1.887)	(−0.061)	
se(*t*-1)				0.033
				(0.507)
se(*t*-2)				0.044
				(0.678)
se(*t*-3)				−0.055
				(−0.870)
R²	0.100	0.173	0.441	0.185
Obs.	168	168	168	168

NOTES: The symbols * (**,***) denote statistical significance at 10 (5, 1) percent level (one- or two-tailed test, as appropriate). See text and notes on table 4.1. The *g* and *s* prefixes refer, respectively, to the goods and service sectors. Metropolitan dummy variables are included in the demand equation; year dummy variables are included in both equations.

the individual sectors were shorter than those estimated for the aggregate. Specifications with longer lag lengths yield roughly similar results. The difference in lag lengths between the aggregate and the sectoral equations is predictable. With interactions between the two sectors, aggregate adjustment will necessarily be longer than the partial adjustment of any one sector.

Turning to the estimates in table 4.2, we find significantly negative wage elasticities of demand for each of the two sectors. The individual demand elasticities for the goods-producing sector are not statistically significant until lag 3, but the cumulative elasticity (-1.751) is significantly negative at the 5 percent level. None of the individual demand elasticities for the service-producing sector are statistically significant, but the cumulative elasticity (-0.227) is significantly negative at the 10 percent level. The significantly greater elasticity (at the 5 percent level) for labor demand in the goods-producing sector could arise for any one of several reasons. For example, the divergence may reflect differences in the price elasticities of demand for the products of both sectors, or greater flexibility in substituting other factors for labor in the goods-producing sector. Both possibilities appear plausible.

Holding the alternative wage constant, we find no significant effect in table 4.2 for employment on the supply wage for either the goods-producing or the service-producing sector, implying that the partial wage elasticity of supply to either one of the sectors is essentially perfectly elastic. However, we do find significantly positive effects in both sectors for the alternative wage.

In the goods-producing sector, the alternative wage (sw) is significantly positive (at the 5 percent level) at lag 3, and the cumulative alternative wage elasticity (0.174) is significantly positive at the 5 percent level. In the service-producing sector, the alternative wage (gw) is significantly positive (at the 1 percent level) at lag 2, and the cumulative alternative wage elasticity (0.306) is significantly positive at the 1 percent level. The effect of the goods-producing sector wage on the service-producing sector supply wage is significantly greater (at the 10 percent level) than the effect of the service-producing sector wage on the goods-producing sector supply wage. This suggests that wage spillovers are greater from the goods-producing sector to the service-producing sector rather than vice versa.

Finally, the backward linkages from the goods sector onto the service sector, reflected by the coefficients on goods employment in the service-sector demand equation, are highly significant, with a cumulative coefficient of 0.206 (significant at the 1 percent level). We view this response as an upper bound, based upon the likelihood that omitted disturbances induce positive correlations in employment between the two sectors.

The specifications in table 4.2 can be extended to include additional interactions between the two sectors. For a subset of our metropolitan-area sample (13 SMSAs), we are able to use local personal income to link the two sectors in both demand and supply. As with the other variables, the income variable is expressed in logarithmic, first-difference form relative to the average. More comprehensive data on income and output in detailed sectors would be even more useful, but are not included here. In labor supply, local personal income is included to obtain income-compensated supply equations. In labor demand, one can use local personal income as a local determinant of the demand for each sector's output (or more accurately for profit-maximizing input demand functions, a determinant of the inverse demand function, or price, for each sector's output).

In labor supply, we find an income elasticity of supply wage of 0.343 (with a t-value of 2.204) for the service-producing sector and of 0.271 (with a t-value of 1.153) for the goods-producing sector. Using very simple discrete lags, we find lags of two and three years, respectively, for the effects of income in the service-producing and goods-producing sectors. Although the income coefficient for the goods-producing sector is statistically insignificant, its value is not significantly less than the income coefficient for the service-producing sector, which is statistically significant and positive at the 5 percent level. Because of this similarity in coefficient values and the strong theoretical presumption regarding the effect of personal income on labor supply, we use both point estimates in the simulations below.

In labor demand, we find a coefficient of 0.271 (with a t-value of 1.318, which is statistically significant at the 10 percent level), on personal income for the service-producing sector, and a coefficient with a t-value of less than 1 for the goods-producing sector. Again, the coefficient on personal income in the labor demand equations should be interpreted as the effect of a shift in the demand (price) of the sector's output on labor demand. Our results suggest that variations in local income do affect the demand for the output of the service-producing sector but not for the goods-producing sector. This conclusion is consistent with the assumption that the output of the goods-producing sector is sold predominantly in external markets.

To close the extended model of interactions between the two sectors, we need an equation determining local personal income. Because we are not interested directly in this equation, we take a relatively simple, reduced-form approach and specify local personal income as a function of past employment and wages in both sectors. Thus, we again use a recursive specification. Metropolitan area and year dummy variables are also included. The estimates of this equation for our subsample of 13 metropolitan areas are presented in table 4.3. The fit of the equation is quite good for first-differences of deviations from an average trend, and the employment variables (service-producing sector employment variables, in particular) are much more significant than the wage variables in determining local personal income. The larger coefficients for service-sector employment, as compared to goods-sector employment reflect the relative size of that sector.

Responses to a Permanent Demand Shock

With the estimates in table 4.2, the estimates of the income coefficients for the subsample of 13 metropolitan areas, and the estimates of the local personal income equation in table 4.3, we are able to simulate the effects of demand and supply shocks on subsectors of a local labor market. Our objectives in examining the two sectors separately are twofold. First, we are obviously interested in the nature of the interactions between the goods-producing and service-producing sectors in both demand and supply. Second, we are also interested in illustrating how these sectoral interactions contribute to the behavior of the overall labor market.

If one ignores all interactions between the two sectors (by setting the income, alternative wage, and goods-sector employment coefficients equal to zero in all equations), a demand shock to a particular sector will have effects only in that sector. These effects are depicted in figures 4.3 and 4.4, respectively, for the goods-producing and service-producing sectors. By ignoring the interactions between the sectors, the effects of a demand shock are virtually immediate, with no substantial over-shooting. The demand shock has little effect on the wage in that sector because the partial elasticity of supply is almost perfectly elastic.

Table 4.3
Estimates of Local Personal Income
(13 cities, t-statistics in parentheses)

Variable	(t)	Lag		
		(t-1)	(t-2)	(t-3)
gw		0.079	0.007	−0.004
		(1.026)	(0.121)	(−0.085)
sw		0.028	0.105**	0.036
		(0.330)	(1.898)	(0.772)
ge		0.030**	0.021*	−0.055**
		(2.268)	(1.636)	(−2.801)
se		0.266***	0.223***	−0.282**
		(3.252)	(2.769)	(−2.162)
intercept	0.011*			
	(1.655)			
R^2	0.713			
Obs.	78			

NOTES: The symbols * (**,***) denote statistical significance at the 10 (5, 1) percent level (one- or two-tailed test, as appropriate). The dependent variable is the first-difference of the logarithm of local personal income, relative to the sample average. The g and s prefixes refer to the goods and service sectors, respectively. Year and city dummy variables are also included in the regression, but omitted from the table for brevity.

Figures 4.5 and 4.6 depict the response of a local labor market to a demand shock to either the goods-producing or service-producing sector, respectively, when interactions between the sectors are reintroduced (that is, permitting the income, alternative wage, and goods-sector employment effects). A demand shock to the goods-producing sector

Figure 4.3
Increase in Goods Sector Labor Demand

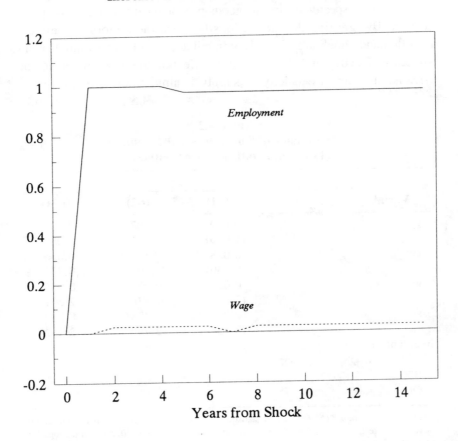

Figure 4.4
Increase in Service Sector Labor Demand

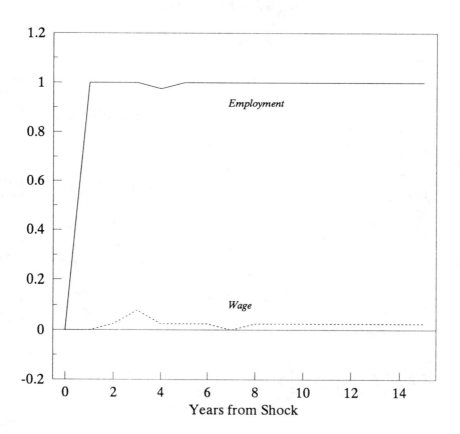

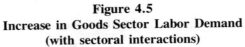

Figure 4.5
Increase in Goods Sector Labor Demand
(with sectoral interactions)

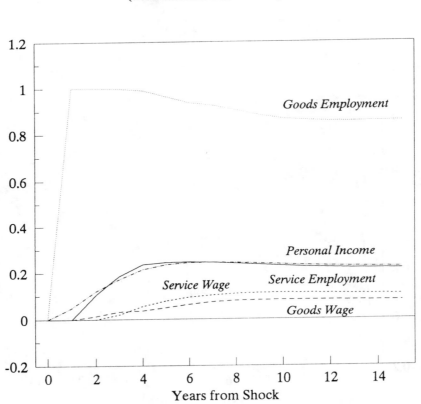

Figure 4.6
Increase in Service Sector Labor Demand
(with sectoral interactions)

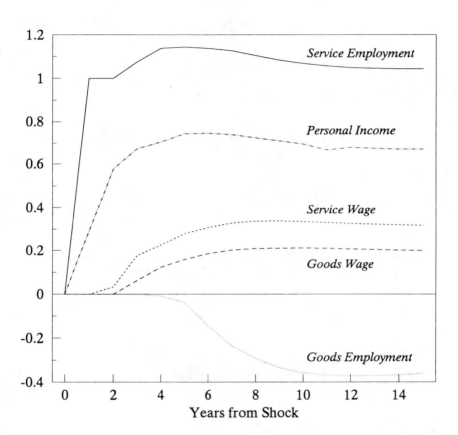

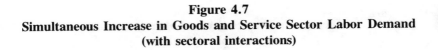

Figure 4.7
Simultaneous Increase in Goods and Service Sector Labor Demand
(with sectoral interactions)

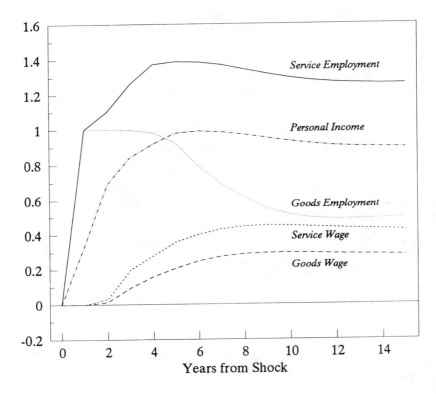

continues to have immediate effects in that sector, modestly positive spillovers onto service-sector employment and local personal income, and very small effects on the wages in either sector. The small spillover effects from the goods to the service sectors suggests that the large multiplier effects often claimed for goods-sector expansions may be confined to the goods sector. That is, an increase in one subsector of the goods sector may have a large effect on the overall goods sector—larger than the analogous case in the service sector.

A demand shock to the service-producing sector generates effects roughly similar to the behavior of the overall market response to a demand shock depicted in figure 4.1. Wages tend to move predominantly with the employment shock, but with some overshooting. There is a slight overshooting for increases in service-sector employment and local personal income, and a decline in goods-sector employment, which results from the induced increase in the goods-sector wage. The employment responses for the two sectors taken together yield an overall response for employment similar to the overall response to a demand shock in figure 4.1. The protracted length of adjustment when the sectoral interactions are included suggests that the job reallocation process between sectors may be a major factor in explaining sluggish adjustment.

The results of a joint demand shock to the two sectors simultaneously are depicted in figure 4.7. Wages, employment, and income tend to overshoot, at least modestly, and the pattern of responses is again quite similar to the overall demand shock in figure 4.1, which adds to our confidence in the subsector results. Demand shocks to the service-producing sector appear to be the most influential in replicating at the disaggregate level the overall pattern of responses to a demand shock at the aggregate level, which may be explained by the fact that the service-producing sector is typically almost three times as large as the goods-producing sector.

Responses to a Permanent Supply Shock

We begin as before by ignoring all the interactions between the two sectors and then introducing a supply shock to either the goods-producing or service-producing sector. The responses are presented in figures 4.8 and 4.9 for the goods-producing and service-producing sectors, respectively. A supply shock to the goods-producing sector causes wages and employment to move predominantly in opposite directions, with about a three-year lag for employment. The adjustment is relatively quick and monotonic, and the employment response is substantially greater than the initial wage change, reflecting the elastic demand for labor in the local goods-producing sector.

The supply shock to the service-producing sector also causes wages and employment to move mainly in opposite directions, with about a two-year lag for employment. The employment response, however, is substantially smaller than the initial wage change, reflecting the inelastic demand for labor in the local service-producing sector. Again, the adjustment is relatively quick and monotonic.

In figures 4.10 and 4.11 we introduce income, alternative wage, and goods-sector employment interactions. For a supply shock to the goods-producing sector, the response with interactions is very similar to the response without interactions, as shown in figure 4.10. However, we now see a modestly positive spillover on service-sector employment and local personal income, and a negative effect on service-sector wages. For the supply shock to the service-producing sector in figure 4.11, we also find similar responses for the service sector with and without interactions, with substantial positive employment spillovers on manufacturing employment and local personal income. The spillover on the goods sector arises largely from the interaction of a small negative spillover on the goods-producing sector wage with the elastic demand for labor in the goods-producing sector.

The results of a joint supply shock to the two sectors simultaneously are depicted in figure 4.12. Compared to the response pattern for the aggregate supply shock in figure 4.2, the pattern in figure 4.12 is qualitatively similar in direction, but does not exhibit the overshooting characteristic of the aggregate responses. The decline in wages in both sectors, the sharp employment rise in the goods-producing sector relative to the service-producing sector, and the slight increase in local personal income appear to be the most salient features of the overall response.

Figure 4.8
Increase in Goods Sector Labor Supply

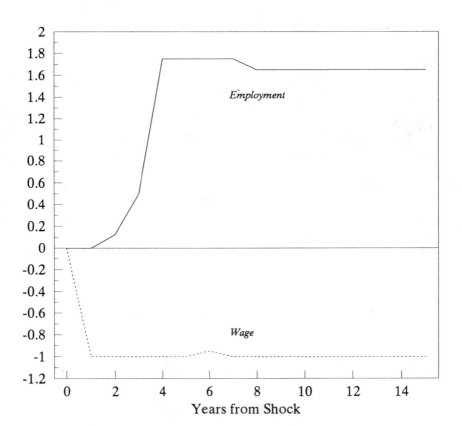

Figure 4.9
Increase in Service Sector Labor Supply

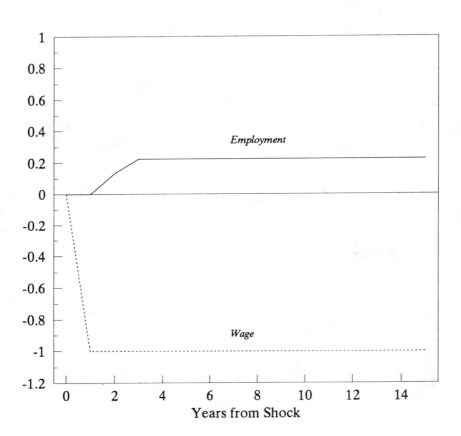

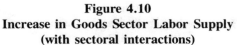

Figure 4.10
Increase in Goods Sector Labor Supply
(with sectoral interactions)

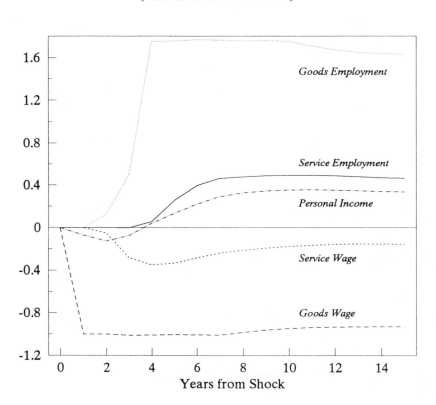

Figure 4.11
Increase in Service Sector Labor Supply
(with sectoral interactions)

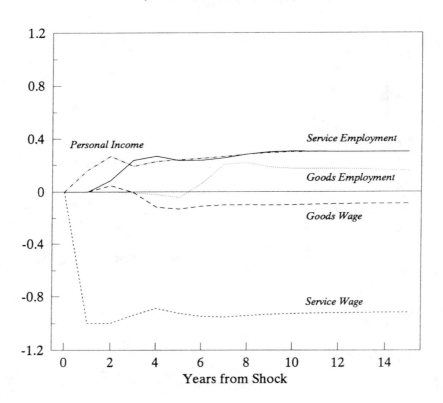

Responses to a Permanent Income Shock

With the structure of the subsector model, we are also able to simulate the response of a local labor market to an exogenous increase in local personal income. One might think of such a shock as, say, an influx of very wealthy retirees, or a sharp increase in (redistributive) state or federal grants to the local government or residents of a particular city. The responses are presented in figure 4.13. By definition, there is a sharp increase in local personal income. This increase raises wages in the goods-producing and service-producing sectors, but the most novel aspect of the response is the sharp drop in employment in the goods-producing sector. This occurs because the increased pressure on the local labor market, reflected in the subsequent rise in wages in both sectors, sharply reduces employment in the goods-producing sector as a result of its elastic demand. In contrast, employment in the service-producing sector rises by almost a quarter.

Conclusion

This chapter has estimated the dynamic relationship between wage and employment and has used these estimates to simulate the labor supply and demand responses to labor market disturbances. The results are consistent with the general sluggishness of wages and employment found in the previous chapter. Simulation results for a representative city, based on data from 21 metropolitan areas during the period 1973 to 1986, show that it takes most of a decade for a metropolitan labor market to return to equilibrium after a disturbance.

However, the road to the new equilibrium is not direct. Labor markets quickly react to the initial disturbance with dramatic swings in employment and wages. A positive demand shock, for example, is met in the very short run by workers offering more hours and unemployed workers finding jobs. However, the short-run response is not enough to alleviate the tight labor market, and wages stay high, although some firms may cut back on demand in response to higher wages. As wages remain high, labor force participation rises as employment opportunities improve.

Figure 4.12
Simultaneous Increase in Goods and Service Sector Supply
(with sectoral interactions)

Figure 4.13
Exogenous Increase in Local Personal Income
(with sectoral interactions)

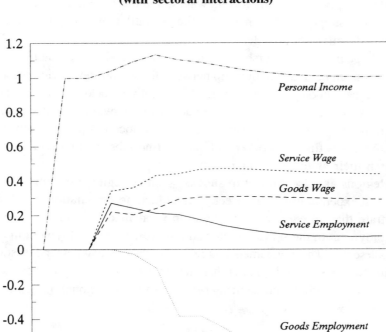

Years from Shock

If the labor market tightness is perceived to be permanent, individuals from outside the region are enticed to move into the area. This increase in labor supply eventually lowers wages, and the shifting back and forth of labor supply and demand continues until a new equilibrium is reached—after about a decade.

A large part of the overshooting and the protracted adjustment response results from the interrelationship between the goods and service subsectors of the economy. For example, when negative shocks hit the manufacturing sector, as they predominantly do, displaced workers seek employment in other sectors. However, the job reallocation process between sectors takes time as workers attempt to find jobs in other sectors that match their skills and preferences.

Regions are also subject to shocks, such as regional distribution of federal expenditures, that directly affect income. Simulation results illustrate that an exogenous increase in local income tends to expand employment in the service sector and to crowd out employment in the goods sector. This phenomenon is related to the fact that demand elasticity in the goods sector is greater than in the service sector—a characteristic that follows from manufacturing selling to a more national market than do services.

NOTE

1. In separate estimates not reported, a contemporaneous wage variable was added to the regression equation. It was not statistically significant and did not affect the estimates of the lagged wage variables, which lends further support for the recursive structure.

5

Local Institutions and Public Policies
Unionization, Taxes, and Public Infrastructure

A host of local institutions and public programs can affect local labor markets. Local institutions, especially labor unions, can alter the labor adjustment process by restricting entry into jobs and occupations and by fixing wages above market levels. On the other hand, labor unions can improve worker skills and workplace safety through apprenticeships and other programs. Other local institutions such as regional trade associations promote the preservation of local industries. Government programs can also influence local labor markets through job-training programs, local educational services, public infrastructure investment, economic development initiatives, and the licensing and regulation of businesses. The effects of these programs include easing difficult labor transitions, improving worker skills, and providing an attractive economic environment for firms and households. The purpose of this chapter is to use the framework established in the last chapter to estimate the influence of these institutions and programs on local labor market adjustment.

We focus on labor unions and local government taxes and expenditures, with particular emphasis on public capital investments. Our selection represents institutions and programs that can directly affect local economic development through their effects on labor demand and supply. Unions are typically seen as imposing high costs on firms. Consequently, firms are reluctant to locate in areas with a strong union tradition unless that area offers site-specific benefits that can offset those costs to the firm. Investment in public capital stock such as roads, highways, and water treatment facilities typically offers businesses a competitive advantage over firms in areas that do not provide the same services at comparable tax costs. While we do not consider the offsetting costs of unions and public capital stock directly, our estimates suggest that unions and infrastructure investment have significant effects on local labor market adjustment.

Unionization and Local Labor Markets

Effect on Overall Supply and Demand

Labor unions can affect both the supply of and the demand for labor. Unions may influence labor supply through apprenticeship programs, hiring halls, or restrictions on entry into certain occupations or industries. Unions, by negotiating wages that are higher than market rates, may also raise the wage expectations of workers, which reduces the number of employed workers in the local labor force. In addition, the generous benefit packages typically negotiated by unions also discourage laid-off workers from seeking employment. The latter effect is seen in many cities that have a strong union tradition but are faced with declining industries.

For example, the demise of the steel industry in Pittsburgh displaced over 50,000 workers during the 1980s. While the unemployment rate rose during this period, indicating that many of these people were actively searching for another job, the labor force participation rate fell at the same time. Workers simply withdrew from the labor force, finding it disadvantageous to seek employment. Older workers took early retirement. Younger laborers depended on union unemployment benefits while waiting for the steel firms to recall their workforces. Most of the companies never did.

On the demand side, a vast literature suggests that labor unions, at least in the decades of the 1960s and 1970s, reduced the level of employment and a firm's ability to adjust employment levels quickly and efficiently to changing market conditions.[1] The restrictions result from wage negotiations that typically keep nominal wages rigid or from work rules and reduction-in-force procedures that prevent employers from adjusting employment levels to the full extent desired. Because of these factors, firms are reluctant to expand or locate within areas with high union representation, consequently reducing the demand for labor.

One view of labor unions as impediments to adjustment follows Mancur Olson's thesis of institutional sclerosis. Labor unions are seen as rent-seeking institutions that endeavor to hold on to the status quo. Steelworker unions, for example, sought to preserve the number of jobs and wage levels that existed before foreign competition shook the industry. The same holds true for many other industries, including textiles and autos. However, in attempting to preserve the status quo, many argue, unions stood in the way of the changes that were necessary to save a particular industry. The higher-than-market wages and the workplace restrictions negotiated by unions raised labor costs that made it more difficult for domestic firms to compete regionally and internationally. The higher labor costs also diverted resources away from capital and research and development investment, which are needed for an industry's long-run viability.

However, some researchers have taken the opposite position and argued that unions actually promote change. Freeman and Medoff (1984), for example, see unions as providing workers with a collective voice. By securing a role in the decisionmaking process, workers can initiate innovations in production processes and in labor-management relations. This position is supported by evidence that in some industries union workers are more productive than nonunion workers.

Considering the effect of unions on the local labor market adjustment process has implications that go beyond the effects of a local institution. It also provides evidence, although indirect, on the relative impact of shocks on union and nonunion workers in an area. If, for example, unions are able to protect their workers from declining wages and increased layoffs during a period when a local labor market is subjected to a negative disturbance, such as appreciably higher oil prices, then some other group may be shouldering a proportionately larger share of the effect. Although we are not able to estimate the relative burden placed on union versus nonunion workers from a shock, the estimates indicate that union affiliation does significantly affect labor market behavior. In this respect, one could infer that shocks affect union and nonunion workers differently.

To examine the relationship between unions and labor supply and demand, we consider two basic effects. The first is the effect of variations in union representation across labor markets on the level of employment or wages. For example, a negative coefficient on the union variable in the demand equation would suggest that areas with higher union representation have lower employment levels, holding wages constant. A positive coefficient on the union variable in the supply equation would indicate that workers in areas of high union affiliation receive higher wages than workers in areas of low union affiliation, even with the level of employment the same.

The second effect relates to the speed and magnitude of adjustment. If the argument holds that unions impede the adjustment process, then one would expect that the elasticity of demand or supply would be lower in areas with higher union representation. The effect of union affiliation on the elasticities is captured by interacting the employment variable with the union variable in the supply equation and the wage variable with the union variable in the demand equation. For example, a positive coefficient on the interaction term in the supply equation could be interpreted to suggest that unions impede the adjustment process, perhaps through their control of the supply of workers. Areas with higher union representation exhibit a lower labor supply elasticity, indicating that employment does not respond as quickly to wage changes, or vice versa. On the demand side, a negative coefficient on the union-wage interaction variable would be consistent with union impediment.

The union-representation variable is taken from the CPS data used to estimate the metropolitan wage differentials. The data are for 1978, which is close to the midpoint of our sample data.[2] We examine variations in the level of unionization because these dominate variations in the trends in unionization for the metropolitan areas in our sample. The other variables are the same ones used in chapter 4, such as year and city dummy variables in the employment equations and year dummy variables in the supply equations.

The regression results with the unionization variables included are presented in table 5.1, where the first column for the demand or supply estimates represents the coefficients for the average level of unionization in our sample, and the second column represents the coefficients for the interaction with the unionization variable. The average proportion of the labor force represented by unions in our sample of metropol-

Table 5.1
Unionization and Local Labor Demand and Supply
(21 cities, t-statistics in parentheses)

Lag/variable	Demand		Supply	
	w(t)	U*w(t)	e(t)	U*e(t)
(t-1)	-0.162***	-0.007	0.212***	0.013**
	(1.753)	(-0.739)	(2.705)	(2.059)
(t-2)	-0.183**	-0.006	-0.040	-0.007
	(-1.848)	(-0.616)	(-0.508)	(-1.121)
(t-3)	-0.270***	0.005	-0.028	-0.006
	(2.982)	(0.683)	(-0.349)	(-0.958)
(t-4)	-0.156**	0.0001	0.285***	0.008
	(-1.944)	(0.008)	(3.540)	(1.121)
(t-5)	-0.326***	0.006	-0.135*	0.003
	(-4.475)	(1.016)	(-1.570)	(0.371)
(t-6)	-0.097*	0.0001	-0.034	-0.005
	(-1.499)	(0.010)	(-0.387)	(-0.705)
U	-0.003***		0.0002	
	(-3.337)		(1.054)	
intercept	0.020		0.012***	
	(1.181)		(2.697)	
R^2	.207		.523	
Obs.	168		168	

NOTES: The symbols * (**, ***) denote statistical significance at the 10 (5, 1) percent level (one- or two-tailed test, as appropriate). Dependent variables are first-differences of logarithms of employment and wages relative to the national average. U refers to the percentage of the local labor force organized, relative to the average.

itan areas is 28 percent in 1978, and ranges from a low of 14 percent to a high of about 47 percent.

In demand, none of the coefficients on the union-wage interaction variables are significant, indicating that unionization is not significantly associated with any differences in the magnitude or speed of adjustment in labor demand. However, the union intercept is significantly negative, suggesting that labor markets with higher-than-average levels of unionization experience declines in employment with wages held constant. Of course, this finding may not be directly attributable to unionization. Many heavily unionized industries have experienced extraordinary declines as a result of a variety of factors, including increased foreign competition and the effects of higher energy prices.

In supply, the coefficient for the union-employment interaction variable at lag 1 is significantly positive at the 5 percent level, indicating that the supply of labor in heavily unionized labor markets is significantly less elastic than in other labor markets. However, this divergence is primarily a short-run phenomenon because the sum over the various lags of the union-employment coefficients (0.006) is not significantly positive. The union-intercept coefficient is also statistically insignificant in the supply equation. As we shall see in the next section, where the goods-producing and service-producing subsectors are examined, the less elastic supply of labor (in the short run, at least) in heavily unionized metropolitan areas may be the result of strong wage spillovers in supply from the goods-producing sector to the service-producing sector.

Effect on Goods and Services Supply and Demand

We also examine the relationship between unionization and the labor demand and supply separately for the goods and service sectors. However, because of the heterogeneity even within the sectors, we cannot be certain that any significant findings for unionization are causal or merely associations resulting from, say, auxiliary correlations between unionization and industry heterogeneity within each sector.

Table 5.2 presents the results of interacting the unionization variable with the labor demand and supply equations of the goods-producing sector. We find that labor demand in heavily unionized metropolitan areas is significantly less elastic than in less unionized areas. For example, for metropolitan areas with one-third less than the average level of union representation, the cumulative wage elasticity of demand is –3.43. For metropolitan areas with one-third more union representation than the average percentage, the cumulative wage elasticity of demand is –0.91, substantially less elastic. The union intercept in labor demand is statistically insignificant.

In the next pair of columns, we find that labor supply in heavily unionized metropolitan areas is also significantly less elastic than in less unionized areas. For metropolitan areas with one-third less union representation than the average, the (implied) cumulative wage elasticity of labor supply is essentially infinite; whereas, for metropolitan areas with one-third more than the average level of unionization, the cumulative wage elasticity of supply is only about 4.2, but is still quite elastic. Unionization does not significantly alter the degree of wage spillover in supply from the service-producing sector because the union interactions with the service-producing sector wage are jointly statistically insignificant. The union-intercept coefficient in supply is also insignificant.

Table 5.3 presents the results of interacting the unionization variable with the labor demand and supply equations for the service-producing sector. Unlike labor demand in the goods-producing sector, labor demand in the service-producing sector is unaffected by the unionization variable. All union interactions and the union-intercept coefficient are significant. There is also no significant effect of unionization on the (implied) wage elasticity of labor supply in the service-producing sector, because the interactions between unionization and employment are jointly insignificant.

There is a significant relationship, however, between unionization and the magnitude of the wage spillover from the goods-producing sector wage to the service-producing sector wage. The coefficients for the interactions between unionization and the goods-producing sector wages (gw) are positive and jointly significant at the 1 percent level. Thus, the greater the degree of unionization in the local labor market, the

Table 5.2
Unionization and Labor Demand and Supply for the Goods-Producing Sector
(21 cities, t-statistics in parentheses)

Lag/variable	Demand		Supply	
	Coeff.	U*Coeff.	Coeff.	U*Coeff.
gw(t-1)	-0.119	0.031		
	(-0.211)	(0.652)		
gw(t-2)	-0.380	0.036		
	(-0.704)	(0.790)		
gw(t-3)	-1.383***	0.072**		
	(-2.904)	(1.813)		
ge(t-1)			0.095***	0.009**
			(2.395)	(2.335)
ge(t-2)			0.001	0.001
			(0.033)	(0.178)
ge(t-3)			0.017	0.004
			(0.425)	(0.915)
sw(t-1)			-0.025	-0.001
			(-0.258)	(-0.141)
sw(t-2)			0.093	-0.007
			(1.119)	(-0.944)
sw(t-3)			0.144**	-0.003
			(1.964)	(-0.426)

U	-0.002	0.0003
	(-0.994)	(1.041)
intercept	-0.015	0.010
	(-0.327)	(1.493)
R^2	0.105	0.232
Obs.	168	168

NOTES: The symbols * (**, ***) denote statistical significance at the 10 (5, 1) percent level (one- or two-tailed test, as appropriate). Dependent variables are first-differences of logarithms of employment and wages relative to the national average. The g and s prefixes refer, respectively, to the goods and service sectors. The dependent variable is $ge(t)$ in demand and $gw(t)$ in supply.

Table 5.3
Unionization and Labor Demand and Supply for the Service-Producing Sector
(21 cities, *t*-statistics in parentheses)

Lag/variable	Demand		Supply	
	Coeff.	U*Coeff.	Coeff.	U*Coeff.
sw(t-1)	-0.093 (-0.955)	0.006 (0.808)		
sw(t-2)	-0.109 (-1.324)	0.006 (0.875)		
sw(t-3)	-0.028 (-0.394)	(-0.001) (-0.233)		
se(t-1)			-0.019 (-0.167)	-0.005 (-0.457)
se(t-2)			0.079 (0.749)	0.001 (0.142)
se(t-3)			-0.091 (-0.926)	-0.005 (-0.522)
ge(t-1)	-.121*** (2.911)	.002 (0.418)		
ge(t-2)	.079** (1.918)	.001 (.232)		
ge(t-3)	-.020 (.519)	-.006 (-1.517)		

gw(t-1)		0.010	0.003
		(0.146)	(0.511)
gw(t-2)		0.174***	0.024***
		(2.545)	(3.693)
gw(t-3)		0.040	0.003
		(0.656)	(0.472)
U	-0.001	0.00003	
	(-.584)	(0.129)	
intercept	0.004	0.014	
	(0.173)	(2.390)	
R^2	0.458	0.273	
Obs.	168	168	

NOTES: The symbols * (**, ***) denote statistical significance at the 10 (5, 1) percent level (one- or two-tailed test, as appropriate). Dependent variables are first-differences of logarithms of employment and wages relative to the national average. The dependent variable is $se(t)$ in demand and $sw(t)$ in supply. The g and s prefixes refer, respectively, to the goods and service sectors.

greater the wage spillover from the goods-producing to the service-producing sectors in labor supply. As with all the other equations, the union-intercept coefficient is statistically insignificant in the equation for the service-producing sector labor supply.

Local Taxes and Public Infrastructure

Overview and Previous Studies

In this section we emphasize the effects of local taxes and local public infrastructure on local labor demand and supply. This analysis touches on two issues related to local labor markets and economic development. The first is the effect of the local fiscal package on regional growth. The second is the stimulative effect of public infrastructure investment on local economies. Both issues have received attention recently from academic researchers and from policymakers, and both issues are still subject to considerable debate.

Theoretical analyses of taxation generally yield ambiguous predictions for the effect on employment and wages unless quite stringent assumptions are imposed. Previous empirical studies of taxes yield no consistent evidence on the effects of taxation on employment, wages, or local economic performance in general. Early studies find no effect of taxation on local economic growth.[3] As surveyed in Due (1961), Stinson (1968), and Oakland (1978), these studies provide no evidence that tax differentials affect any measure of local economic performance. This conclusion has been rationalized by arguing that local (and state) taxes on business are relatively small as compared to the total costs of production, and that interregional tax differentials are also relatively small as compared to other cost differences, such as transportation.

More recent empirical studies offer mixed results. One group continues to find no significant effect for local or state tax differentials.[4] However, a second group of studies does find significant effects for tax differentials. As demonstrated by Mofidi and Stone (1990), one explanation for the divergent results between the two groups of studies is the treatment of the expenditure side of local and state public finance.

When major expenditure categories for a particular level of government are controlled, the results of tax differentials become more predictable. In particular, when expenditures on what are usually considered public goods are held constant (expenditures, for example, on public infrastructure, education, community health, and police and fire protection), higher taxes are usually associated with lower growth, lower employment, lower wages, and lower public investment.

Most of the previous studies noted above examine state-level data. Here, we seek to reexamine these issues in the context of metropolitan areas, which coincide much more closely with local labor markets. Our raw measure of taxes is total local tax revenues (net of intergovernmental transfers) and comes from the Census of Governments and the intervening Survey of Governments. To obtain an implicit aggregate local tax rate we express this measure relative to local personal income. As with employment and wages, we express the tax ratio in logarithmic, first-difference form relative to the average.

Our focus on the expenditure side of local governments is with the local public capital stock. Recent attention has been given to the role of investments in highways, roads, bridges, sewers, and water treatment facilities on local economic development. In part, this attention is spurred by the eroding quantity and quality of public infrastructure in many older, industrial cities, as well as by the inadequate growth of public infrastructure in some cities that have experienced rapid growth in the last decade or so. Until recently, it was impossible to formally test hypotheses related to the public capital stock, because of the lack of public capital stock estimates. Estimates now exist for a sample of metropolitan areas and states, and these estimates will be used in this chapter.[5]

In labor demand, the local public capital stock can be viewed as an unpaid factor of production that enhances the productivity of labor and/or private capital. To illustrate this concept, consider transportation infrastructure, such as a network of roads and highways. Transportation services are undoubtedly fundamental to a firm's production process. Without transportation, the flow of inputs into a plant and the shipment of products out would not be possible. Moreover, markets could not exist without the physical means of bringing producers and consumers together. An increase in the stock of highways and streets would then increase the quantity of transportation services available to firms. Areas with a well-developed and maintained highway system offer firms an advantage over businesses in areas lacking that infrastructure, assuming the same tax liabilities. Therefore, one would expect that infrastructure attracts firms, raising employment levels.

Transportation services may have indirect effects on a company's productivity by enhancing the productivity of other inputs. For example, the accessibility of workers to their workplace is a growing problem in urbanized areas. As workers spend more time commuting, they may be inclined to work fewer hours, and the hours actually spent on the job may be less productive because of the energy and aggravation spent getting to and from work. In addition, highway (and mass transit) congestion, coupled with poor transportation systems to accommodate commuting patterns, limits the pool of workers for some business establishments. For example, several studies have documented the problem faced by poorer households in urban areas in finding convenient public transportation to the service and manufacturing jobs that increasingly locate in suburbs.

The semiconductor industry in the Silicon Valley is a graphic example of the effects of an inefficient transportation system.[6] As housing prices in the northern part of the valley escalated, production workers in the industry, who were typically lower paid than engineers, were forced to find homes further away from the production facilities, commuting longer distances, and leading in part to greater traffic congestion. The reduction in the labor pool immediately around the plants increased labor costs, and eventually forced much of the production side of the semiconductor industry to leave the area. An efficient transportation network would probably have helped to hold down labor costs and keep facilities in the region.

In labor supply, public infrastructure may also affect household migration decisions by enhancing an area's amenities. The local public capital stock can be thought of as a subsidy to private consumption of a partially public good or an expansion of positively valued local amenities. Existing literature related to household location decisions addresses only minimally the effects of public infrastructure. Labor migration studies tend to concentrate primarily on demographic characteristics and wage differentials to explain migration flows. Urban quality-of-life comparisons, which deal with the same underlying decision process, come closer to addressing this issue, but their major focus is on attributes such as air quality, climate, and so forth.

To account for these effects, an infrastructure variable is entered into the labor demand and labor supply equations. Unlike the case with unionization, we do not expect infrastructure to influence labor elasticities, and thus we do not interact infrastructure with the wage variables or employment variables. For our analysis we express local public capital stock in logarithmic, first-difference form relative to the average.

This study uses estimates of public capital stock for a sample of metropolitan areas between 1958 and 1987. Public capital stock includes roads, streets, bridges, water treatment and distribution systems, waterways, airports, and mass transit.[7] We follow the standard method of measuring capital stock, which is to use the monetary approach, often referred to as the "perpetual inventory technique." The measure of capital under this method is the sum of the value of past capital purchases adjusted for depreciation and discard. The result is a stock of public capital for any given year that incorporates the accumulation of past annual public investments, minus the replacement of existing capital stock.

Estimates

Table 5.4 presents our estimates of the effects of local tax rate differentials and the local public capital stock on local labor demand and supply. As with our analysis of local personal income earlier, we are limited by data to a subsample of 13 metropolitan areas. For simplicity, we choose the single most significant lag for each variable. For the tax variable (t), the most significant lag is 2 in demand and 4 in supply. For the public capital stock variable (k), the most significant lag is 3 in both demand and supply. However, for a stock variable, the lag structure is unimportant, since it represents an accumulation of many years of annual investments. Also for simplicity, only the cumulative coefficients for the wage and employment variables are presented.

Table 5.4
Taxes, Public Infrastructure, and Local Labor
Demand and Supply Equations
(1973–87, 13 cities)

Variable	Labor demand	Labor supply
intercept	–0.022*** (–3.257)	0.012*** (2.484)
w(t-1) to w(t-6)	–0.576*** (–3.687)	
e(t-1) to e(t-6)		0.390*** (4.387)
t(t-i)	–0.049** (–1.972)	0.033** (1.673)
k(t-i)	0.346** (1.862)	–0.318** (–2.252)
R^2	0.221	0.247
Obs.	104	104

NOTES: The symbols * (**,***) denote statistical significance at the 10 (5, 1) percent level (one- or two-tailed test, as appropriate). Dependent variables are first-differences of the logarithms of employment and wages, respectively, relative to the national average. The variables t and k are first-differences of the logarithms of the ratio of tax revenues to personal income and the local public capital stock, respectively, relative to the sample average. Lags are indicated in parentheses beside each variable. For taxes i is 2 in labor demand and 4 in labor supply. For the public capital stock i is 3 in both equations. See text for sources and details.

Examining the results, we find that the coefficient for the tax rate variable is significantly negative in labor demand and significantly positive in labor supply, as expected. These significant coefficients suggest that, with the local public infrastructure held constant, increases in local tax rates tend, on average, to reduce both local labor demand and supply. The coefficient for the local public capital stock is significantly positive in labor demand and significantly negative in local labor supply, as expected. These estimates, taken together, strongly support the argument made by Mofidi and Stone (1990) that the total fiscal package (both taxes *and* expenditures) is the appropriate yardstick with which to gauge the effect of taxes or expenditures on regional growth.

Since taxes pay for government services, and government services are valued by firms and households, the relative efficiency of provision and the appropriate mix of services are the relevant consideration. For example, areas that offer the same government services (in this case, public infrastructure), but at a higher cost to taxpayers, will in general be less attractive to firms and households, since the costs to firms and households are higher. The same holds true for areas with the same tax liabilities, but different levels of public services. Obviously, if the tax burden is not equally shared by firms and households, benefits are transferred to the sector (e.g., households or firms) that has the lower tax share or that consumes the larger share of public services.

The estimates related to public infrastructure provide particularly strong support for the notion that local public capital stock is important in the location decisions of firms and households. The positive relationship between infrastructure and employment, holding wages constant, suggests that areas with larger-than-average infrastructure development are able to attract firms, presumably because infrastructure enhances a firm's productivity. These results are consistent with those of Eberts' (1991) that show that public infrastructure is positively associated with the percentage of jobs gained in a region through business openings.

The negative sign on the public infrastructure variable in the supply equation also supports the positive benefits of infrastructure, but this time with respect to households. Areas with higher-than-average infrastructure investment, holding taxes constant, are able to attract households in the area. This subsequently increases labor supply and lowers wages.

One can also explain the negative effect of infrastructure on wages in terms of compensating wage differentials. Households in regions with higher-than-average public capital stock, everything else including taxes and wages the same, are better off than their counterparts in areas with less capital stock. These households in the high-investment area would, consequently, be willing to accept lower wages until their total well-being (from higher infrastructure consumption and lower wages) equaled the total well-being of individuals elsewhere, with lower infrastructure consumption but higher wages. Thus, the results suggest that households positively value public infrastructure.

Conclusion

The operation of local labor markets is influenced by local institutions and local government tax and expenditure policies. In this chapter we focused on labor unions, taxes, and public infrastructure. Estimates based on the framework described in the previous chapter reveal that these three factors have significant effects on local labor markets. They primarily affected the levels of wages and employment, in ways that we expected.

Unions exhibited their largest effects in lowering the demand for labor in local economies and in slowing the speed of adjustment in goods-producing sectors, which are typically the most heavily unionized industries. They slowed the speed of adjustment of both demand and supply for the goods-producing sectors. This, in turn, spilled over to the service sector. The restrictive effect of unions on the goods-producing sector of cities has important implications for the response of cities to business cycle shocks. Since goods-producing sectors are much more cyclical than service-producing sectors, the union impediment to adjustment extends the length of time required for local labor markets to fully return to equilibrium.

Local government tax and expenditure policies also significantly affect local labor markets. Our results are consistent with the general wisdom that higher taxes deter employment growth and reduce supply, if there are no differences across regions in other factors. Results also showed that public infrastructure is an important input of firms and an important consumption good for consumers. Therefore, those areas that excel in infrastructure development will also be attractive to households and firms, which spurs regional growth.

These results underscore the long-term benefits of public infrastructure investment, and, conversely, warn against public expenditure packages that neglect basic elements of regional growth, such as public infrastructure, in order to meet short-term problems.

It seems as if many cities find themselves in a vicious circle with regard to public infrastructure and economic development. Cities, particularly those with an aging industrial base, often find that they cannot afford to maintain or improve their infrastructure because of heavy demand for welfare programs and the decline in the tax base caused by a sagging local economy. Evidence in this chapter of the importance of infrastructure to firms and households suggests that the longer public works improvements are neglected, the harder it will be to break the cycle between deteriorating infrastructure and economic development.

NOTES

1. Although Holzer and Montgomery (1990) found no difference in wage and employment variability between union and nonunion firms, other studies reported in Hirsch and Addison (1986), for example, have documented differences in wage and employment levels.

2. The year 1980 is the actual midpoint, but the unionization variable is not available in the CPS data for the years 1979 to 1982.

3. These studies include Floyd (1962), Bloom (1955), Thompson and Mattila (1959), Fuchs (1962), Perloff and Dobbs (1963), and Williams (1967).

4. These studies include Morgan and Brownlee (1974), Morgan and Hackbart (1974), Mulkey (1976), Vasquez and deSeve (1977), Adams et al. (1979), Hodge (1979), Kieschsnick (1981), Schmenner (1982), and Carlton (1983).

5. The metropolitan public capital stock series was constructed by Randall W. Eberts, Michael S. Fogarty, and Gaspar Garofalo, under a grant from the National Science Foundation. State-level estimates have been constructed by Alicia Munnell of the Federal Reserve Bank of Boston.

6. See Saxenian (1984).

7. A more detailed description of the public capital stock data, along with an application of the data to the issue of regional economic productivity, is provided by Eberts (1986).

6

Conclusions

We began our study by raising basic questions about wage and employment determination in local labor markets. What are the major components of shifts in local labor supply and demand? How persistent are metropolitan differences in wages and unemployment rates? How strong are demand and supply responses for labor in major metropolitan markets? How long do these responses take? How do local labor markets respond when disturbed from equilibrium? Do demand or supply shocks tend to dominate observed changes in wages and employment? Are there important differences in the behavior of the major subsectors of a local labor market? How do these subsectors interact? Do variations in the extent of unionization affect the behavior of local demand and supply? Do major local public policies (tax rates and investments in local public infrastructure, in particular) influence local wage and employment determination?

We raised these questions because local demand and supply functions for labor are poorly understood, reflecting the paucity of empirical research at the local level. In addition, evaluation of the influence of local public policies on wages and employment is based on a very inadequate knowledge base, in some instances only on "folklore." While there is some detailed evidence on the effects of local training and income-maintenance programs, there is little reliable evidence on the effects of broad policies dealing with tax rates and investments in public infrastructure, such as highways, roads, bridges, lighting, sewers, water treatment, airports, mass transit, parks and recreation facilities, public hospitals, community health clinics, and educational facilities.

To obtain answers, it was first necessary to acquire data on wages, worker skills and other attributes, employment, unemployment rates, unionization rates, income, taxes, and public infrastructure for a sample of metropolitan areas. Next, we used a recursive structure to separate demand and supply responses. The combination on the one hand of novel data and on the other of the power of the recursive specification in identifying demand and supply enabled us to obtain answers to the basic questions raised above.

What are these answers? We find that the largest, most immediate component of shifts in local labor supply in recent years has been changes in labor force participation, rather than changes in unemployment rates or migration. Over time, however, migration plays an increasingly important, and ultimately dominant, role. The largest, most immediate component of change in local labor demand has been variation in the openings of new firms, rather than in closings, expansions, or contractions. This stands in sharp contrast to the popular impression that regions decline primarily as a result of closings in declining industries, and stands as a warning to policymakers who focus primarily on the special requests of declining industries at the expense of appropriate general economic policies.

For the local labor market as a whole, we find that wage differentials among metropolitan areas are much more persistent over time than unemployment rate differentials, which tend to erode over periods as short as a decade. Our evidence also supports previous findings of a recursive structure in local labor supply and demand, where firms initially adjust employment rather than wages in response to economic disturbances.

Estimates of local labor supply and demand based upon this recursive structure are elastic, but protracted: adjustment of a local labor market to a relatively broad supply or demand shock, for example, occurs over a period in excess of a decade. In addition, there is a tendency for both wages and employment in the local labor market to overshoot— to move too far before turning back toward their new equilibrium values. Although demand shocks appear, on average, to have dominated wage and employment patterns in local labor markets during the period we examined, supply shocks have also been important.

At a more disaggregated level, we find that for the goods- and service-producing sectors of local economies, demand for labor is more elastic in the goods sector than in the service sector. This finding is consistent both with our expectation and our evidence that the demand for goods sector output is less dependent on local factors than the demand for service sector output. Our estimates also imply that the partial wage elasticity of labor supply to either the goods or service sector is essentially infinite, but that wage spillovers from one sector to the other are significant in labor supply for both sectors, particularly so for spillovers from the goods sector to the service sector. Our simulation of the effects of an exogenous increase in local income indicates that such increases appear to sharply reduce goods-sector employment by driving up local wages.

With regard to unionization, we find that both labor demand and supply in the goods sector is much less elastic in heavily unionized cities. Cities with unionization rates one-third higher than the average have an elasticity of labor demand in the goods sector of only about one-fourth that of cities with unionization rates one-third lower than the average. For labor supply in the goods sector, the divergence is even greater. For the service sector, however, we find no difference in elasticities in either labor demand or supply with variations in the level of unionization. We do find, as one might expect, that wage spillovers in supply from the goods sector to the service sector are more significant in heavily unionized cities.

Finally, we also find significant evidence bearing on the crucial issues related to local tax policies and investments in local public infrastructure. For our measure of local tax rates, we find that increases in tax rates tend to reduce both local labor demand and supply, with lags of several years. For local public infrastructure, broadly defined to include such investments as parks, public hospitals, and community health clinics, as well as roads, sewers, and bridges, we find that increases in the local public capital stock tend to increase both local labor demand and supply, also with lags of several years. These findings offer support to those arguing for a "back-to-basics" approach to local public policy, but should also disquiet those arguing that a low tax policy, per se, is the most effective policy for encouraging local economic growth.

The political horizon at the local level is often only as far as the next election, but the adjustment horizon for the local labor market is at least a decade. This mismatch leads to two related problems. First, the protracted adjustment period itself, especially with overshooting, often requires policymakers to deal with the most immediate consequences of an economic downturn through increased expenditures on social welfare programs and, as a consequence, increased taxes. However, the increased taxes and decreased share of public expenditure going toward public infrastructure, police and fire protection, and local schools places the local economy at a long-term competitive disadvantage—a sort of vicious circle. Second, the most basic policies to improve the competitive position of a local economy take longer to yield tangible benefits than the average political horizon. Thus, for both reasons, the protracted adjustment horizon for local labor markets poses special problems for policymakers. For this reason, there may be a role for state and/or federal policies to diminish the tendency toward vicious circles and encourage wise local investments to promote long-term growth.

APPENDIX
Description of Data and Methodology

This appendix describes the data used to construct wage and employment estimates. Because the wage information is obtained from responses of individuals to the *Current Population Survey* (CPS) compiled by the Bureau of Labor Statistics, considerable attention is given to the nature of this dataset and the methods that we used to construct a standardized wage for metropolitan areas. In particular, we offer a detailed discussion of how metropolitan wages are adjusted for differences in skill levels across metropolitan areas so we can compare the wage differential of a typical worker in each of the local labor markets.

CPS Files

CPS surveys from 1973 to 1987 are used in this analysis. Various features of the CPS files have changed over the years we cover, which introduces several problems when using these data to derive consistent time series of metropolitan area wages.

First, the method of collecting wage and worker characteristics has changed. For the years 1973 through 1978, questions regarding worker wages and characteristics were asked in only one month—May. This poses two problems. The first is that the sample contains only those individuals who were in the second rotation, which reduces the number of respondents. The second problem is that annual wage estimates will reflect wages obtained for only one month of the year.

Starting in 1979, the wage questions were asked of one quarter of the individuals in each of the 12 monthly surveys conducted each year. Because of the difference in the way in which information is gathered, the total number of workers with sufficiently complete records for analysis is much smaller before 1979 than afterward. For instance, the 1974 CPS contains 40,792 workers, while the 1983 CPS includes 175,268 workers.

The second change has to do with boundary definitions of urban areas. Unlike some other government agencies that gradually changed the definitions of metropolitan areas over time when urban areas grew or shrank significantly, BLS maintained the same SMSA definitions until 1985. In 1985, they decided to adopt new classifications that replaced SMSAs with Metropolitan Statistical Areas (MSAs) and Primary Metropolitan Statistical Areas (PMSAs). This new policy brought about abrupt changes in the size of metropolitan areas, par-

131

ticularly those that experienced rapid growth. Of the 43 metropolitan areas that are identified on the CPS files, 27 had boundary changes after 1985.

BLS also changed the metropolitan boundary definitions when constructing employment series from their *Employment and Earnings* files. These changes proved to be the more formidable when constructing employment series than the wage series. Employment series for many of the more rapidly growing cities jumped dramatically after 1985 when counties were added to the existing metropolitan area. We found no satisfactory way of dealing with this problem, except to use in the analysis only those metropolitan areas that had no boundary changes throughout the entire 15-year period. This reduced the usable number of metropolitan areas from 46 to 21. These metropolitan areas are listed in table A.1 by broad geographic areas. Of the four major divisions, only the South is poorly represented. As we will show later in the discussion of employment, the sample is fairly evenly distributed between SMSAs experiencing employment growth over the period and those experiencing employment decline.

Table A.1
List of SMSAs Included in the Analysis by Major Regions

Northeast	Midwest	South	West
New York	Detroit	Miami	Los Angeles
Philadelphia	Cleveland		San Francisco
Nassau—Suffolk	Milwaukee		Anaheim
Rochester	Cincinnati		San Diego
	Indianapolis		Denver
	Columbus		San Bernardino-
	Akron		Riverside
	Gary–Hammond		Sacramento
			San Jose

The third change has to do with the union question. In the May survey, workers were typically asked whether or not they were union members. However, from 1979 through 1982, workers were no longer asked about their union affiliation. This omission became a problem when relating the local labor market dynamics to union concentration.

Skill-Adjusted Metropolitan Wage Differentials

Skill-adjusted wage differentials are obtained from the coefficients of metropolitan dummy variables included in a wage equation that also contains variables reflecting observed determinants of worker productivity. Following the human capital specification of Hanoch (1967) and Mincer (1974), we specify individual wages (expressed in logarithms) as a function of the worker's education level (entered as a quadratic); potential experience (age, minus years of education, minus six, also entered as a quadratic); the interaction between experience and female, binary dummy variables indicating full-time employment status, female, nonwhite, and 46 occupation dummy variables. Detailed information on other components of labor compensation (for example, pensions and health insurance) is not available on the CPS files. Union membership status and industry dummy variables are not included because these variables are not viewed as productive attributes.

The wage differential between two metropolitan areas, obtained in this way, can be interpreted as the difference in wages that two identical workers could earn in these two markets. The difference is presumably due to labor market conditions, both demand and supply, and not due to differences in the skills possessed by workers in their respective labor forces.

Two assumptions are made in using this technique. First, we assume that the worker characteristic variables and the occupation variables capture all the productivity attributes of the individual workers, so that the metropolitan dummy variables only reflect wage differentials due to differences in local labor market conditions. Second, we assume that the effect of worker attributes on wages is the same across all metropolitan areas. To test this second assumption, we could interact each of the worker-characteristics variables with the dummy variables. Unfortunately, the small sample size for most of the metropolitan areas does not allow us to do this.

It is interesting to note that the difference between the actual metropolitan wage differentials and the skill-adjusted ones is the difference in the value of skills embodied in each respective labor market. This can be seen by separating the wage differential between metropolitan areas into two components: differences in the skill-adjusted wages; and differences in the value of skills (measured in dollars).

Figure A.1 depicts the difference in actual wages between two SMSAs (w_A and w_B). The relationship between wages (shown on the vertical axis) and a skill index (shown on the horizontal axis) is captured by the slopes of the two lines—one line for city A and the other for city B. Notice that the wage level in city A (the upper line) embodies a higher skill level than the wage in city B (the lower line). Therefore, a portion of the wage differential between cities (w_A-w_B) is due to differences in skills. If the skill level of each city is forced to be the same, then the resulting wage differential could be thought of as the difference in wages that an identical worker (in terms of skills) could receive between the two labor markets.

134

Figure A.1
Components of Metropolitan Wage Differentials

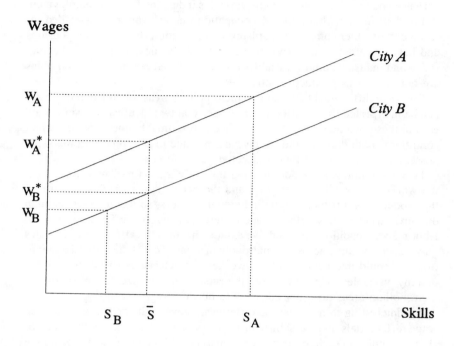

This skill-adjusted intermetropolitan wage differential is measured by the vertical distance between the two lines at some fixed level of skills. This difference is depicted in figure A.1 as $w^*_A - w^*_B$. The difference in wages between city A and city B due to differences in skills is then represented by the addition of the two line segments: $w^*_A w_A$ and $w^*_B w_B$.

Wage Regressions

Wage regressions were estimated for each of the 15 years. Although the primary purpose for estimating these wage equations is to derive skill-adjusted wage differentials for metropolitan areas, it is interesting to examine the effect of various worker characteristics on wages. Table A.2 contains the coefficient estimates associated with race, sex, schooling, and experience for representative years. The results from the other years are very similar as illustrated by charts showing the trends of those coefficients over time. All of the worker-characteristics variables enter with the expected signs. These coefficients are statistically significant at the 1 percent level, except schooling squared for a few years.

Table A.2
Wage Equation Estimates for Selected Years, 1973 and 1987

	1973		1987	
Variable	Parameter estimate	t-statistic	Parameter estimate	t-statistic
Full-time	0.131	21.136	0.194	70.592
Nonwhite	-0.047	-6.518	-0.063	-21.357
Female	-0.204	-26.050	-0.119	-34.662
Experience	0.028	55.647	0.030	119.512
Experience squared	-0.0004	-43.222	-0.0004	-85.777
Schooling	0.145	18.164	0.168	37.944
Schooling squared	0.001	0.914	-0.003	-3.173
Experience *Female	-0.005	-16.766	-0.005	-36.841
R^2	.90		.96	
Obs.	40,792		179,341	

SOURCE: CPS files for selected years.

Full-time employees (who work 35 hours or more a week) receive higher wages than part-time workers, everything else the same. This full-time wage premium has increased from 12 percent in 1973 to almost 20 percent in 1987. This fairly sizable increase has occurred even though the percentage of full-time workers has remained constant.

The nonwhite wage differential has also changed significantly over the 15-year period. The wage gap between nonwhite and white employees narrowed between 1974 and 1978, falling from 5.8 percent in 1974 to 3.4 percent in 1978. However, from 1983 to 1987 the wage gap widened, and in 1987 nonwhites were paid 6.3 percent less than otherwise comparable white employees, the largest differential in the 15-year period. This increase in the nonwhite differential has taken place as the percentage of nonwhite employees has grown from 10 to 13 percent of total employment.

The female wage differential, on the other hand, has narrowed over time. In 1973, female workers were paid 30 percent less on average than males with similar qualifications. By 1987, this gap had narrowed to 21 percent. During that period, female workers' share of total employment had increased slightly to around 48 percent.

The schooling variable is measured in discrete terms in order to capture the discontinuities in the potential effect of grade school, high school, and college education on earnings. School is entered with a value equal to 1 for 8 to 11 years of education, a value of 2 for 12 to 15 years, a value of 3 for 16 to 17 years, and a value of 4 for more than 18 years. In addition, schooling squared is entered to account for additional nonlinearities in the effect of education on wages.

The net effect of schooling on wages, after taking into account possible nonlinearities, is displayed in figure A.8. The effect of schooling on wages remained virtually constant during the 1970s, but took a discernible drop in 1979. Although the effect of schooling on earnings has trended upward in recent years, its impact in the late 1980s is still about the same as it was in the 1970s. This rather constant effect in the face of apparent increases in the need for more highly trained workers may be partly explained by the relatively greater abundance of more highly educated workers in the 1980s than in the 1970s.

The net effect of experience on earnings was also considered in the wage regression. Unfortunately, CPS does not contain exact measures of a worker's experience. Researchers typically approximate the years of experience by assuming that the worker began employment immediately after completing his or her formal education, assuming that everyone entered first grade at age six. In this way, experience is proxied by subtracting years of education (plus six) from the age of the worker. Experience squared is entered to pick up nonlinear relationships between experience and earnings. Experience is also interacted with the female variable in order to take into account the fact that females' careers are typically interrupted by child-rearing activities, and thus experience as calculated does not capture the entry and exit from the labor force.

The experience of workers has declined slightly over the last 15 years, reflecting the movement of the baby-boom cohort into the labor market.

Also included in the regression are 46 occupation dummy variables, which help to control for skill differentials that may be specific to occupations. With the executive/professional occupation omitted from the wage regression, all but one or two of the occupation coefficients are statistically significant each year.

Estimates of Metropolitan Wage Differentials

As mentioned earlier, the purpose of estimating the wage equations is to derive skill-adjusted wage differentials for our sample of 21 metropolitan areas. The wage differentials are obtained from the estimated coefficients associated with the dummy variables for each metropolitan area identified in the CPS. We also included separate dummy variables to identify workers in metropolitan areas that were not individually identified and to identify workers in nonmetropolitan areas. The national average wage was then subtracted from the SMSA dummy variable estimates so that the metropolitan wage differentials could be interpreted as deviations from the national wage rate.

Goods-Producing and Service-Producing
Sector Wage Differentials

Separate wage differentials were also estimated for the goods-producing and service-producing sectors of each SMSA. The goods-producing sector includes (1) construction and (2) manufacturing. The service-producing sector includes (1) transportation, communications, and public utilities; (2) wholesale and retail trade; (3) finance, insurance, and real estate; (4) services; and (5) government.

Metropolitan wage differentials for these broadly defined sectors were estimated using the same technique as described above. The wage differentials for the two sectors are obtained by interacting SMSA dummy variables with dummy variables that identified a worker as being employed in either a goods-producing or a service-producing industry. The same worker characteristics are included in these individual sector wage regressions as those which appeared in the regressions used to estimate average wage differentials for all sectors.

Employment

The employment levels for each SMSA are obtained from *Employment and Earnings*. State employment agencies estimate nonagricultural employment by sampling employers within their states every month. These data are gathered under rigid guidelines set forth by the Bureau of Labor Statistics, which also compiles the data to derive national employment estimates. The sample of workers includes persons who worked during, or received pay for, any part of pay periods which include the twelfth of the month. Excluded from the sample are proprietors, the self-employed, unpaid family workers, farm workers, and domestic workers. In order to be consistent with the wage data from the CPS, we used May employment figures to construct annual time-series data. As mentioned earlier, because of the significant changes in metropolitan boundary definitions, only 21 of the possible 46 SMSAs for which wage data are available yielded consistent employment time series.

Table A.3
Percentage Employment Changes Between 1973 and 1987

Metropolitan area	Total	Goods	Services
Gary–Hammond	6.32	--	--
Cleveland	2.75	-28.1	20.6
Akron	3.62	-26.5	23.5
New York	3.71	-30.3	13.4
Detroit	10.44	-21.8	32.3
Milwaukee	15.31	-17.0	35.0
Philadelphia	16.94	-20.3	34.9
Rochester	21.16	-8.7	43.5
Cincinnati	26.89	-6.6	45.1
San Francisco	28.09	2.9	32.6
Indianapolis	32.54	-8.6	52.7
Los Angeles	32.64	13.4	41.2
Denver	33.35	-10.5	47.8
Columbus	33.42	-9.3	51.0
Miami	37.26	-2.6	49.5
Nassau–Suffolk	43.08	18.1	51.6
San Jose	77.42	73.8	79.6
Sacramento	77.52	82.7	76.8
San Bernardino–Riverside	81.03	71.4	83.9
San Diego	90.00	76.8	93.7
Anaheim	105.75	68.2	125.9

SOURCE: Bureau of Labor Statistics, *Employment and Earnings.*

Total employment in all of the 21 SMSAs, except Gary-Hammond, has increased over the last 15 years. As expected, most of this growth, especially in recent years, has been in the service-producing sectors. All of the 21 SMSAs had significantly more employment in services in 1987 than in 1973. Anaheim registered the largest gain with a 125 percent increase between 1973 and 1987. New York's 13 percent increase was the smallest gain. Employment in the goods-producing sectors increased in this 15-year period in only 8 of the 21 SMSAs. All of the gains but one (Nassau-Suffolk) occurred in California cities. The largest losses (in percentage terms) were experienced by New York, Cleveland, and Akron, in that order.

References

Abraham, Katharine G., and Lawrence F. Katz. 1986. "Cyclical Unemployment: Sectoral Shifts or Aggregate Disturbances?" *Journal of Political Economy* 94 (3): 507-22.

Adams, Jack E., Dale M. Lewison, and Convay T. Rucks. 1979. "Public Industrial Location Inducements: Snowbelt-Sunbelt Preferences," *Review of Regional Economics and Business* (October): 3340.

Adams, James D. 1985. "Permanent Differences in Unemployment and Permanent Wage Differentials," *Quarterly Journal of Economics* (February): 29-53.

Baldwin, John, and Paul Gorecki. 1990. *Structural Change and the Adjustment Process: Perspectives on Firm Growth and Worker Turnover,* Ottawa, Canada: Canadian Government Publishing Centre.

Bartik, Timothy J. 1990. "The Distributional Effects of State and Local Economic Development Policies." Presented at the Association for Public Policy Analysis and Management, San Francisco, October.

Bauer, Paul W., and Susan M. Byrne. 1991. "The Sectoral and Regional Effects of Oil Price Shocks: Who's Over a Barrel?" *Economic Commentary,* Federal Reserve Bank of Cleveland, January 15.

Beeson, Patricia E., and Randall W. Eberts. 1987. "Identifying Amenity and Productivity Cities Using Wage and Rent Differentials," *Economic Review,* Federal Reserve Bank of Cleveland, Quarter 3.

_____. 1989. "Identifying Productivity and Amenity Effects in Interurban Wage Differentials," *Review of Economics and Statistics* 71 (August): 443-52.

Bloom, Clark. 1955. "State and Local Tax Differentials," Iowa City: Bureau of Business Research, State University of Iowa.

Brown, James N. 1982. "How Close to an Auction is the Labor Market? Employee Risk Aversion, Income Uncertainty, and Optimal Labor Contracts." In *Research in Labor Economics,* vol. 5, ed. Ronald G. Ehrenberg. Greenwich, CT: JAI Press.

Carlton, Dennis. 1983. "The Location and Employment Choices of New Firms: An Econometric Model with Direct and Continuous Endogenous Variables," *Review of Economics and Statistics* (August): 440-49.

Charney, Alberto. 1983. "Introduction to Manufacturing Location Decision and Local Tax Differentials," *Journal of Urban Economics* 14: 184-205.

Davis, Steve J., and John C. Haltiwanger. 1990. "Gross Job Creation and Destruction: Microeconomic Evidence and Macroeconomic Implications," *NBER Macroeconomics Annual* 5: 123-68.

Due, J.T. 1961. "Studies of State-Local Tax Influences on Location of Industry," *National Tax Journal* 14: 163-73.

141

Dunne, Timothy, Mark J. Roberts, and Larry Samuelson. 1989. "Plant Turnover and Gross Employment Flows in the U.S. Manufacturing Sector," *Journal of Labor Economics* 7 (1): 48-71.

Eberts, Randall W. 1986. "Estimating the Contribution of Urban Public Infrastructure to Regional Growth." Working Paper 8610, Federal Reserve Bank of Cleveland, December.

_____. 1989. "Accounting for the Recent Divergence of Regional Wage Differentials," *Economic Review,* Federal Reserve Bank of Cleveland, Quarter 3.

_____. 1990a. "Cross-Sectional Analysis of Public Infrastructure and Regional Productivity Growth." Working Paper 9004, Federal Reserve Bank of Cleveland, May.

_____. 1990b. "Can State Employment Declines Foretell National Business Cycles?" *Economic Commentary,* Federal Reserve Bank of Cleveland, September 15.

_____. 1991. "Some Empirical Evidence on the Linkage Between Public Infrastructure and Local Economic Development." In *Industry Location and Public Policy,* ed. Henry W. Herzog, Jr. and Alan M. Schlottmann. Knoxville, TN: University of Tennessee Press.

Eberts, Randall W., and Timothy J. Gronberg. 1991. "Wagner's Hypothesis: A Local Perspective." Working Paper, Federal Reserve Bank of Cleveland.

Ecker, Deborah S., and Richard F. Syron. 1979. "Personal Taxes and Interstate Competition for High Technology Industries," *New England Economic Review* (September/October): 25-31.

Eichengreen, Barry. 1986. "Currency Union," *Economic Policy* (April).

Evans, G. 1986. "The Conduct of Monetary Policy and the Natural Rate of Unemployment." Working Paper, Stanford University.

Flaim, Paul O., and Ellen Sehgal. 1985. "Displaced Workers of 1979-1983: How Well Have They Fared?" *Monthly Labor Review* 108 (June): 3-16.

Floyd, Joe S., Jr. 1962. *Effects of Taxation on Industrial Location.* Chapel Hill: University of North Carolina Press.

Fox, William. 1981. "Fiscal Differentials and Industrial Location: Some Empirical Results," *Urban Studies* 18: 105-11.

Freeman, Richard B., and James L. Medoff. 1984. *What Do Unions Do?* New York: Basic Books.

Fuchs, Victor. 1962. *Changes in the Location of Manufacturing in the U.S. Since 1929.* New Haven: Yale University Press.

Gallaway, Lowell, Richard Vedder, and Robert Lawson. 1991. "Why People Work: An Examination of Interstate Variations in Labor Force Participation," *Journal of Labor Research* 12 (1)(Winter).

Gerking, Shelby D., and William N. Weirick. 1983. "Compensating Differences and Interregional Wage Differentials," *Review of Economics and Statistics* 65 (August): 483-87.

Greenwood, Michael J. 1975. "Research on Internal Migration in the United States: A Survey," *Journal of Economic Literature* 13 (2): 397-433.

Greenwood, Michael J., Gary L. Hunt, Dan S. Rickman, and George I. Treyz. 1990. "Migration, Regional Equilibrium, and the Estimation of Compensating Differentials," Working Paper, Department of Economics, University of Colorado.

Groshen, Erica L. 1991. "Sources of Intra-Industry Wage Dispersion: How Much Do Employers Matter?" *Quarterly Journal of Economics* (August).

Hall, Robert E. 1970. "Why is the Unemployment Rate So High at Full Employment?" *Brookings Papers on Economic Activity* 3: 369-402.

Hamilton, James D. 1983. "Oil and the Macroeconomy Since World War II," *Journal of Political Economy* 91 (April): 228-48.

Hanoch, Giora. 1967. "An Economic Analysis of Earnings and Schooling," *Journal of Human Resources* 2 (3): 310-29.

Hanushek, Eric A. 1979. "Alternative Models of Earnings Determination and Labor Market Structure," *Journal of Human Resources* 16 (2): 238-59.

Haynes, Stephen E. 1988. "Identification of Interest Rates and International Capital Flows," *Review of Economics and Statistics* 70 (1).

Haynes, Stephen E. and Joe A. Stone. 1985. "A Neglected Method of Separating Demand and Supply," *Journal of Business and Economic Statistics* 3 (3): 238-43.

Helms, L. J. 1985. "The Effect of State and Local Taxes on Economic Growth: A Time Series-Cross Section Approach," *Review of Economics and Statistics* (November): 574-82.

Hirsch, Barry T., and John T. Addison. 1986. *The Economic Analysis of Unions: New Approaches and Evidence.* Boston: Allen and Unwin.

Hodge, J. 1979. "A Study of Regional Investment Decisions," Ph.D. dissertation, University of Chicago.

Holzer, Harry J., and Edward B. Montgomery. 1990. "Asymmetries and Rigidities in Wage Adjustments by Firms," Working Paper No. 3274, National Bureau of Economic Research, March.

Houseman, Susan N., and Katharine G. Abraham. 1990. "Regional Labor Market Responses to Demand Shocks: A Comparison of the United States and West Germany." Paper presented at the Association for Public Policy Analysis and Management, San Francisco, October.

Hulten, Charles R., and Robert M. Schwab. 1984. "Regional Productivity Growth in U.S. Manufacturing: 1951-1978," *American Economic Review* 74 (March): 152-62.

_____. 1991. "Public Capital Formation and the Growth of Regional Manufacturing Industries." Paper presented at the Conference on the Economics of Tax-Exempt Bond Markets, National Bureau of Economic Research, Annapolis, April 6.

Jacobson, Louis. 1986. "Job Creation and Destruction in Pennsylvania, 1975-1985." Mimeo. W.E. Upjohn Institute for Employment Research, Kalamazoo, MI, November.

Kieschsnick, Michael. 1981. *Taxes and Growth: Business Incentives and Economic Development.* Washington, DC: Council of State Planning Agencies.

Kniesner, Thomas J., and Arthur H. Goldsmith. 1987. "A Survey of Alternative Models of the Aggregate U.S. Labor Market, *Journal of Economic Literature* 25 (September): 1241-81.

Lawrence, Robert Z. 1984. *Can America Compete?* Washington, DC: The Brookings Institution.

Leonard, Jonathan S. 1987. "In the Wrong Place at the Wrong Time: The Extent of Frictional and Structural Unemployment." In *Unemployment and the Structure of Labor Markets,* ed. Kevin Lang and Jonathan S. Leonard. New York: Blackwell.

Lilien, David M. 1982. "Sectoral Shifts and Cyclical Unemployment," *Journal of Political Economy* 90 (August): 777-93.

Markusen, Ann. 1988. "Government as Market: Industrial Location in the U.S. Defense Industry." Working Paper, Center for Urban Affairs and Policy Research, Northwestern University, April.

Marston, Stephen T. 1985. "Two Views of the Geographic Distribution of Unemployment," *Quarterly Journal of Economics* (February): 57-79.

Mincer, Jacob. 1974. *Schooling, Experience, and Learning.* New York: Columbia University Press.

Mofidi, Ala. 1988. "Taxes, Expenditures, and State Economic Performance." Ph.D. dissertation, University of Oregon.

Mofidi, Ala, and Joe A. Stone. 1990. "Do State and Local Taxes Affect Economic Growth?" *Review of Economics and Statistics* 72 (November): 686-91.

Morgan, W. Douglas, and Elliot Brownlee. 1974. "The Impact of State and Local Taxation on Industrial Location: A New Measure for the Great Lakes Region," *Quarterly Review of Economics and Business* (Spring): 67-77.

Morgan, W. Douglas, and M. M. Hackbart. 1974. "An Analysis of State and Local Industrial Tax Exemption Programs," *Southern Economic Journal* (October): 200-05.

Mulkey, David, and B. L. Dillman. 1976. "Location Effects of State and Local Industrial Development Subsidies," *Growth and Change* (April): 37-43.

Murphy, Kevin M., and Robert H. Topel. 1987. "The Evolution of Unemployment in the United States: 1968-1985." Unpublished manuscript, University of Chicago.

Newman. Robert J. 1983. "Industry Migration and Growth in the South," *Review of Economics and Statistics* (February): 76-86.

Oakland, W. H. 1978. "Local Taxes and Intra-Urban Industrial Location: A Survey." In *Metropolitan Financing and Growth Management*, ed. George Break. Madison: University of Wisconsin.

Ohio's Third Century, Meeting the Economic Challenge Through Science and Technology. A Report of the Ohio Science and Technology Commission.

Olson, Mancur. 1982. *The Rise and Decline of Nations,* New Haven: Yale University Press.

Perloff, Harvey S., and Vera W. Dobbs. 1963. "How a Region Grows." Supplementary Paper No. 17, Committee for Economic Development, Washington, DC, March.

Pissarides, Christopher A., and Ian McMaster. 1990. "Regional Migration, Wages and Unemployment: Empirical Evidence and Implications for Policy," *Oxford Economic Papers* 42: 812-31.

Roback, Jennifer. 1982. "Wages, Rents, and Quality of Life," *Journal of Political Economy* 90 (6): 1257-78.

Rosen, Sherwin, ed. 1981. *Studies in Labor Markets.* Chicago: University of Chicago Press.

Sahling, Leonard G., and Sharon P. Smith. 1983. "Regional Wage Differentials: Has the South Risen Again?" *Review of Economics and Statistics* 65 (February): 131-35.

Saxenian, Annalee. 1984. "The Urban Contradictions of Silicon Valley: Regional Growth and the Restructuring of the Semiconductor Industry." In *Sunbelt and Snowbelt: Urban Development and Regional Restructuring,* ed. Larry Sawers and William K. Tabb. Oxford: Oxford University Press.

Schmenner, R. W. 1982. *Making Business Location Decisions,* Englewood Cliffs, NJ: Prentice Hall.

Segal, David. 1976. "Are There Returns to Scale in City Size?" *Review of Economics and Statistics* 53: 339-50.

Stinson, Thomas F. 1968. "The Effects of Taxes and Public Finance Programs on Local Industrial Development: A Survey of the Literature," *Agricultural Economic Report No. 133,* U.S. Department of Agriculture.

Thompson, Wilbur R., and John M. Mattila. 1959. *An Econometric Model of Postwar State Industrial Development.* Detroit: Wayne State University Press.

Topel, Robert H. 1986. "Local Labor Markets," *Journal of Political Economy* 94 (3): S111-43.

Van Dijk, Jouke, Hendrik Folmer, Henry W. Herzog, Jr., and Alan M. Schlottmann. 1989a. "Labor Market Institutions and the Efficiency of Interregional Migration: A Cross Country Comparison." In *Migration and Labor Market Adjustment,* ed. Jouke Van Dijk, Hendrik Folmer, Henry W. Herzog, Jr., and Alan M. Schlottmann. Dordrecht, The Netherlands: Kluwer.

_____. 1989b. *Migration and Labor Market Adjustment.* Dordrecht, The Netherlands: Kluwer.

Vanderkamp, John. 1989. "The Role of Migration in Regional Adjustment." In *Migration and Labor Market Adjustment,* ed. Jouke Van Dijk, Hendrik Folmer, Henry W. Herzog, Jr., and Alan M. Schlottmann. Dordrecht, The Netherlands: Kluwer.

Vasquez, Thomas, and Charles W. deSeve. 1977. "State/Local Taxes and Jurisdictional Shifts in Corporate Business Activity: The Complications of Measurement," *National Tax Journal* (September): 285-97.

Wasylenko, Michael. 1980. "Evidence on Fiscal Differentials and Intrametropolitan Firm Location," *Land Economics* 56: 339-49.

Wasylenko, Michael, and Therese McGuire. 1985. "Jobs and Taxes: The Effect of Business Climate on States' Employment," *National Tax Journal* (December): 497-511.

Williams, William V. 1967. "A Measure of the Impact of State and Local Taxes on Industry Location," *Journal of Regional Science* 7: 49-59.

Index

152

Sahling, Leonard G., 73n9
Samuelson, Larry, 46n7, 68
Saxenian, Annalee, 11n3, 125n6
Schmenner, R. W., 125n4
Schwab, Robert M., 49, 73n2
Sehgal, Ellen, 11n1, 19, 72
Services sector
    elasticity of labor supply and demand in, 10, 86-90, 106, 129
    estimates of wage elasticites in, 86-90
    labor union effect on, 112-18
    response to demand and supply shocks of, 90-102
Shocks. *See* Economic shocks
Smith, Sharon P., 73n9
SMSAs. *See* Standard Metropolitan Statistical Areas (SMSAs)
Solow residuals, 49
Standard Metropolitan Statistical Areas (SMSAs), 23, 25, 131
Stinson, Thomas F., 118
Stone, Joe A., 73n7, 76, 80, 118, 122

Tax policy, 124
Tax structure
    as economic shock, 56
    effect on labor supply and demand of, 11
    effect on wage differentiation of, 63
    impact of state and local, 53, 56, 118-25
    See also Capital stock, public; Government spending; Infrastructure, public
Technological change as economic shock, 48-50
Thompson, Wilbur R., 125n3
Topel, Robert H., 19, 65, 76, 81
Trade associations, 107

Unemployment rates
    differences in metropolitan, 66-71
    measurement of regional, 25-26, 27
    persistence of, 65-66, 68
    relationship to wages of, 71-73
U. S. Department of Commerce
    Bureau of Economic Analysis, 24t, 28t, 54-55t
    Bureau of the Census, 54-55t
U. S. Department of Labor, Bureau of Labor Statistics (BLS), 24t, 28t, 39f, 40f, 41f,
        43f, 67t, 131, 138t
U. S. Small Business Administration, 35t, 36t

Vanderkamp, John, 22
Van Dijk, Jouke, 21, 46n2